UNCIVIL WARS

❧

Men, Women & Office Etiquette in the 90s

by
Beverly H. Patrick

KENDALL/HUNT PUBLISHING COMPANY
4050 Westmark Drive   Dubuque, Iowa 52002

Illustrations by Melanie Smith.

Copyright © 1994 by Beverly H. Patrick

ISBN 0-8403-9261-3

Printed in the United States of America

10   9   8   7   6   5   4   3   2   1

IN APPRECIATION TO

❧

*My husband, Gordon Patrick,
Melanie Smith and Carol Hebenstreit*

FOREWORD

Beverly Patrick takes a common-sense, no-nonsense approach to the kinds of healthy attitudes and good manners that are necessary for success, personally and professionally, in today's world. Her down-to-earth approach makes it easy to apply these proven guidelines to success.

Treating one another with kindness, decency, and consideration is the basis of her book. And that philosophy is the foundation for any successful relationship.

Abigail Van Buren

Abigail Van Buren
February 22, 1994

PREFACE

Why Manners Still Matter

I f you've ever found yourself at a meeting with your dress tucked in your panty hose—or your fly open, as the case may be—well, you know something about humility. That's the spirit I bring to manners. It's a subject I wouldn't dare talk about if I'd never made a fool of myself.

But manners *and* business? On first blush, they seem to go together like tea cozies and fist fights. Still, despite the old, unpleasant images that many of us carry of stuffed shirts and wagging fingers, manners are more relevant than ever in the workplace. Especially where men and women are concerned.

Not long after the Clarence Thomas/Anita Hill episode, a male colleague said, "I feel like Rip Van Winkle! I wake up and there are all these new rules. Now will somebody please tell me what the rules are?"

But that's the beauty of manners. While we wrangle out the new seating arrangements, good manners are still crystal clear to men and women alike. If nothing else, they're about basic decency, much like the kid on the commercial who—not knowing what better to do—offers the visiting extraterrestrial a Pepsi. Just be decent and you'll do all right.

No, manners won't stop problem people or sexual harassers. On the other hand, I *have* seen major collisions between well-intentioned men and women that could have been avoided if people had known (or at least observed) some basic rules of the road.

And maybe manners aren't so much about putting our best foot forward but rather our *humanness* forward-most. You see, no one is so exalted or famous as to be beyond manners. Man or woman, CEO or street sweeper, today we *all* go first.

Enjoy!

Beverly H. Patrick

CONTENTS

DECENCY IS IRRESISTIBLE

Manners: The Oldest Form of Risk Management

"The keynote to manners is what the French call la politesse du coeur . . . perhaps no manners are really good without a kind heart."

MODERN MANNERS AND THE UNMANNERLY AGE.

Mrs. George Cornwallis-West, *The Cosmopolitan*, 1904.

Civility costs nothing and buys everything.

—LADY MARY WORTLY MONTAGU (1756)

The first quality of a good education is good manners—and some people flunk the course.

—HUBERT H. HUMPHREY (1967)

Manners. Say the word and most people think of something associated with food. Use "manners" as a Password clue and nine people out of ten shoot back "table." Manners means place settings with a lot of complicated silverware. Manners means "Don't chew with your mouth full!" "Place your napkin on your lap." "Don't begin until everyone is served!" Remember the old "Manners the Butler" TV commercials? That "Manners" sold napkins. Manners means food.

Etiquette. That suggests the protocol of receiving lines or seating arrangements or something to do with weddings. Etiquette means the proper way to write an invitation, or have one printed, or respond to one. Sometimes etiquette refers to the arcane determinants of proper dress—black tie? white tie? dinner jacket? long dress? short dress? casual dress? Those are the images that come to mind when we hear the word "etiquette."

And what about *courtesy*? Courtesy is most often used in regard to dealings between men and women. Who holds doors open for whom is courtesy. Helping someone put on a coat is courtesy. Which one walks on which side of the street. Courtesy is most often associated with what men do for women.

Manners, etiquette, courtesy. One runs into the other and they all run together. Good manners may be common sense, but in my experience good manners are far from common. Many expert definitions have been offered as to what good manners really are:

* P.J. O'Rourke in *Modern Manners*: "Good manners consist of doing precisely what everyone thinks should be done, especially when no one knows quite what that is."

* Mark Twain: "Good manners consist of concealing how much we think of ourselves and how little we think of others."

❖ Fred Astaire: "The hardest job kids face today is learning good manners without seeing any."

Today's media at least seem to have reached something of a consensus on the subject of good manners: they hardly exist any more. Pick up any newspaper or magazine and you're likely to see a news item or columnist polemic decrying the sorry state of American manners.

In a syndicated column entitled "More Civil Rights, Less Civility," Ellen Goodman contrasts the bounty of new laws and court rulings that empower minorities to extract compensation for the slightest of slights with the absence of laws mandating decent conduct between human beings. "Civil rights protects individuals. Civility protects the community. Individuals plead their own case in court. Who pleads for the community?"

In a *Washington Business Journal* article entitled "Common Sense and the Good Old Days," John R. Brinkerhoff bemoans "a world in which Madonna, Andrew Dice Clay, Ice T, and Beavis and Butt-Head are cultural icons [where] it is hard to preach the common sense virtues of moderation and courtesy . . . What is needed is a resurgence of common sense based on doing what is right. Civility and courtesy need to be applied in the workplace."

During the 1993 election campaign, the *New York Times* ran a half-page story on a long-shot candidate for the obscure position of a suburban town clerk. Why? Because in the classic man-bites-dog formula 21-year-old Pamela Bednarik was "the very model for civic decency." Her deeds of decency included praising one opponent's rendition of the national anthem, wishing all her opponents good luck, and apologizing for characterizing the incumbent clerk's office as "bloated." (Unfortunately, she lost the election anyway.)

Even Barney the purple-and-green PBS dinosaur has been drawn into the debate. In a story entitled "Of Love, Civility, And Other Dinosaurs," *Washington Post* columnist Steve Twomey assails the Barney backlash of parents who condemn the character as cloying, insipid, and altogether nauseating. "It's just marvelous that in a nation with rampant violence on its streets and televisions, some of us can belittle a character whose message to little people is gentleness, *who teaches them civility.*"

Of course, all this furor is about social and general societal manners. But manners and business? On first blush they seem to go together about as well as tea cozies and fist fights. Still, despite the old unpleasant images of stuffed shirts and wagging fingers, manners are more relevant than ever in the workplace.

Good business manners are signs of professionalism. Unless you're in a profession where oafishness and crudeness are distinct assets—and I'm afraid only professional wrestling comes to mind—polished manners and a command of business etiquette are certain to help you get along with the people you work with and boost your career.

Personal Business Manners IQ Test

Are you a manners genius? My "course" on manners and business—which really isn't a world-class oxymoron—begins with the quiz I give the audience at my presentations. Take a moment to see how you score.

1. In the last three months have you:
   a) Been offended by an off-color joke told in the office? ☐ Yes ☐ No
   b) Not told an off-color joke? ☐ Yes ☐ No
   c) Been offended by swearing in the office? ☐ Yes ☐ No
   d) Not sworn in the office? ☐ Yes ☐ No

2. Do you always feel properly dressed for meetings? ☐ Yes ☐ No

3. In the last three months have you:
   a) Praised a co-worker? ☐ Yes ☐ No
   b) Praised your supervisor? ☐ Yes ☐ No
   c) Apologized to a co-worker or supervisor? ☐ Yes ☐ No
   d) Sent a handwritten thank-you note to a:
   • Co-worker? ☐ Yes ☐ No
   • Client? ☐ Yes ☐ No
   • Supervisor? ☐ Yes ☐ No
   • Colleague? ☐ Yes ☐ No

5. During lunch/dinner/drinks with colleagues or clients do you:
   a) Stand when someone arrives at the table? ☐ Yes ☐ No
   b) As host, instruct the server to take your guests' orders first? ☐ Yes ☐ No
   c) Ask to be excused when leaving the table during the meal? ☐ Yes ☐ No
   d) Put your napkin on the chair when leaving the table? ☐ Yes ☐ No

6. Do you stand when a visitor enters your office? ☐ Yes ☐ No

7. When you tour your workplace with a visitor do you:
   a) Introduce your visitor to staff along the tour? ☐ Yes ☐ No
   b) Use full names when making introductions? ☐ Yes ☐ No

Scoring

Each *yes* is worth five points. Your score: _____ Yes × 5 = _____

Summary

95–110 *Genius Level.* The business world needs more of you.

75–90 *Extremely Bright.* Room for improvement but keep up the good work.

50–70 *Average.* Your sense of business etiquette needs further development.

30–45 *Borderline.* If you want to succeed in the business world, take a close look at your behavior in the workplace.

0–25 *Manners-Disabled.* Remedial training strongly recommended. However, the situation is not hopeless. Reading this book is the first step toward recovery.

Use the same point and rating system to test your company's mores and policies.

Business Manners IQ Test for Your Company

1. Does your company have:
   a) A written dress code? ☐ Yes ☐ No
   b) An unwritten dress code instead of or in addition to a written code? ☐ Yes ☐ No
   c) Is either policy enforced? ☐ Yes ☐ No

2. Is proper dress the norm for:
   a) Men? ☐ Yes ☐ No
   b) Women? ☐ Yes ☐ No

3. Does your company have a written policy on sexual harassment? ☐ Yes ☐ No

4. Does your company have a policy regulating the solicitation of contributions for:
   a) Wedding, baby shower, birthday presents? ☐ Yes ☐ No
   b) Charity drives, girl scout cookies, etc.? ☐ Yes ☐ No
   c) Tupperware, Amway, etc.? ☐ Yes ☐ No

5. Does your company have a policy that clearly states words or phrases that are forbidden in the office?
   a) Written policy? ☐ Yes ☐ No
   b) Unwritten policy instead of or in addition to a written code? ☐ Yes ☐ No
   c) Whether written or unwritten, is the policy enforced? ☐ Yes ☐ No

6. Does your company have a policy on intra-office romance?
    a) Written policy?   ☐ Yes   ☐ No
    b) Unwritten policy?   ☐ Yes   ☐ No
7. At your office are doors held open for:
    a) Women?   ☐ Yes   ☐ No
    b) Men?   ☐ Yes   ☐ No
8. Does your company have a policy on:
    a) Handling phone messages?   ☐ Yes   ☐ No
    b) Greeting visitors to the office?   ☐ Yes   ☐ No
    c) Use of E-Mail?   ☐ Yes   ☐ No
    d) Smoking?   ☐ Yes   ☐ No
9. In your company:
    a) Do you address your supervisor by his/her last name?   ☐ Yes   ☐ No
    b) Does your superior address you by your last name?   ☐ Yes   ☐ No

How does *your* company shape up? Whose manners are better, your employer's or yours? If you're like most people I know, and work at a place that's like most companies I know, chances are good both can use some improvement. Chances are also pretty good that you're not absolutely sure what concepts like manners, etiquette, and courtesy are really all about.

❧❧❧

Let's take a look at the origin of business manners. They didn't evolve just to convey happy thoughts or snappy sentiments. Very polite language can be used to facilitate very impolite discourse. Take the language used in Congress or Parliament. Think about how prefacing a statement with "my learned colleague" or "the esteemed gentleman from South Carolina" takes some of the sting out of violent disagreements.

At one time we were all very primitive people fighting with one another. Manners evolved as a form of defense. In olden days, for example, a handshake signaled that you were not about to draw your sword.

Manners like these became the first forms of risk management. My background in insurance is all about risk management—managing the risk of doing business. All businesses today, large and small, have to be concerned with risk management. Why not let manners be the first line of defense in *your* risk management program?

The good business manners discussed in this book are founded upon two very basic and simple premises:

1. Everyone in business—subordinates, peers, superiors, clients, competitors—should be treated courteously, respectfully, decently.
2. The rules of etiquette are exactly the same for men and women.

From this starting point, the exact rules change from industry to industry, company to company, department to department. The dress code in the insurance industry, for example, is more formal than the dress code in the publishing industry. Walk the halls of an advertising agency and you can't help but notice the difference between account executives—classic conservative suits—and "creative" people—wild colors, flamboyant designs, whatever style is trendy and hot.

Listen for language codes, too. You seldom hear a profane or obscene syllable in a bank, but a newspaper office is no place for "virgin ears."

Mastering the company's rules of etiquette—the written and spoken ones as well as the unwritten and unspoken ones—is a major challenge for new employees. The rules may seem confusing, complex, contradictory because they're mostly based on customs and conventions that evolved long before the new hire arrived on the scene. Usually, however, the company code is based on common sense and quickly mastered.

The best advice I can offer to new employees: Watch what people do; listen to what co-workers say; pay attention to what they don't say. For example, if you go through your first week on the job without hearing a single four-letter word, chances are swearing violates the unwritten/unspoken code and trailblazing verbal indelicacies will not be appreciated.

Manners are of even more vital concern for managers. Look at the qualities of good managers. Good managers respond to all questions politely and patiently. Good managers listen carefully when others are speaking to them. Good managers are prompt, attentive, responsible, thoughtful, professional. Good managers have good manners.

Do good manners guarantee success in business? Certainly not. But I guarantee that good manners improve the chances for success of anyone who has them.

The Japanese have the world's best manners and most rigid code of etiquette. Japan has in less than 50 years since it was nearly destroyed in the second World War turned itself into the world's second largest manufacturing power. Is there a connection?

H. Wayne Huizenga, the self-made chairman of Blockbuster Entertainment and part-owner of the Miami Dolphins, Florida Marlins, Republic Pictures, and dozens of other high-profile entertainment companies, has legendary wealth and legendary manners. A *New York Times* profile made a point out of how Huizenga always grabs the uncomfortable middle seat of cars and personally serves guests in his home or stadium boxes. Huizenga is worth an estimated $700 million. Is there a connection?

The point is that people who are considerate, thoughtful, courteous, and decent can also be phenomenally successful. Good manners *are* good business.

Good business manners are even more important where men and women are concerned. Not long after the Clarence Thomas/Anita Hill episode, a male colleague said, "I feel like Rip Van Winkle! I wake up and there are all these new rules. Now will somebody tell me what the rules are?"

Indeed, as far as men-women '90s workplace relationships are concerned, it's not clear what constitutes good behavior. It's like driving at night down a dark road with no center line. But what it's *really* about is trust. As a very attractive female colleague of mine put it, "It's extremely difficult to look at a man with respect and take him seriously when his eyes are focussed 12 inches below your chin."

One of the principal goals of this book is to iron out some rough spots between men and women in the workplace. From my experience, the best way to do that is through the gentle power of manners. While men and women grope for position in the workplace, good manners are still crystal clear to men and women alike. If nothing else, they're about basic decency—much like the kid on the commercial who, not knowing what else to do, offers the extraterrestrial a Pepsi. Just be decent and you'll do all right.

Good manners are genderless and generationless. They can't be patented, copyrighted, or franchised. Those who possess good manners would make them freely available to poachers, plagiarists, counterfeiters, trademark infringers, and thieves.

Why are good manners still the oldest, best, and cheapest form of risk management? Because they can prevent clashes from ever happening. No,

GOOD MANNERS ARE GENDERLESS AND GENERATIONLESS.

manners won't stop problem people or make sexual harassers see the light. On the other hand, I *have* seen major collisions between well-meaning men and women that could have been avoided if people had followed some basic rules of the road.

I'll close this chapter with three key thematic points that figure prominently in our examination of the *Uncivil Wars* in the workplace of the '90s.

1. ***Good manners are still the best safety valve.*** In a changing and volatile workplace, decency *is* irresistible—could *you* ever resist it? We're human beings first, men and women second.

2. ***Good manners are gender blind.*** Don't open doors for women; open them for people. Extend everyone equal amounts of thoughtfulness and courtesy.

3. ***Separate your professional life and social life.*** Don't presume on business associates. Don't bring personal problems to the office. Don't make co-workers double as parents, siblings, or unpaid therapists. Draw a line between work and the rest of your life. The line is called *professionalism.*

YOU'VE COME A LONG WAY—MAYBE

A Close Look at Today's "Gender-Neutral" Workplace

When the day comes that the American Express Company has to hire a female employee, it will close its doors.

—JAMES CONGDELL FARGO, PRESIDENT OF AMERICAN EXPRESS, 1881–1914

When men had the executive suite pretty much to themselves, everyone knew their place; the rules were rigid and well understood. Today all that has changed.

—LETITIA BALDRIDGE (1993)

he office of today is a far different place from the one I entered in 1957. The most obvious difference was the smoking. At that time smoking was more than just acceptable, it was the norm. Office workers could smoke wherever and whenever they pleased: at their desks, at your desk, in any meeting, even in elevators.

Everybody in the office smoked—except the women. Men were allowed to smoke in the office; women were not. As Ross Perot would say, it was that simple.

Times have changed: Now *not* smoking has literally become the rule in the American workplace of today. Syndicated columnist Ellen Goodman observes, "Public smoking, like public spitting, is becoming a socially unacceptable habit." Workplace smokers of every gender are consigned to dim smoking lounges or forced to leave the building entirely.

Doing Business in the United States, a no-nonsense orientation guide for visiting foreign executives, points out that "smoking has gone from an acceptable, 'sophisticated' activity, to one which is greeted by an increasing number of people with contempt . . . Many office and government buildings do not permit smoking or restrict it to certain designated areas."

I would hasten to advise foreign (and domestic) businesspeople that, even in offices where smoking is not banned, it would be considered a serious breach of courtesy to light up before obtaining full-hearted permission from their host. Moreover, the absence of an ashtray in proximity to the smoking hand strongly suggests that such permission will be granted only grudgingly or quite possibly refused.

Smoking is actually a relatively insignificant change in American workplace manners. Dramatically more significant alterations are necessary due to the changing nature of the cast of characters. Almost every one of the smokers I encountered in the office I entered in 1957 was white and he was male. Individually, they were very different sorts of men, but culturally they were very much in the same boat.

Today's workplace is a much more diverse place. Anecdotal evidence of this is available in the conspicuous presence of women, African-Americans, Hispanics, and Asians you can observe in every office or factory in the country. Statistical evidence comes from the U.S. Labor Department, which reports that 45% of the total U.S. work force are women, 13% are African-American, and 10% are of Hispanic origin. Furthermore, *Workforce 2000*, a study by the Hudson Institute, predicts that by the year 2000 U.S.-born white men will constitute only 15% of the U.S. work force. Native white women will represent the lion's share (42%), and other major components will be native nonwhite women (13%), native nonwhite men (7%), non-native men (13%), and non-native women (9%).

Changing workplace demographics are also reflected by no less a barometer of social change than *New Yorker* cartoons. In 1991 *The New Yorker* published 14 cartoons depicting boardroom meetings—a staple setting for ridiculing the follies of big business—and they included six white women, five black men, and one black women. In 1981, by contrast, the magazine's 20 boardroom cartoons included only three women and no minorities of either gender at all.

There are women in law offices, women in courts as reporters and interpreters, women in the stock exchange, women editors, women directors—women in every conceivable branch of art, industry, and commerce.

—LILLIAN EICHLER, *BOOK OF ETIQUETTE* (1923)

The workplace change that occasions the biggest shift in workplace manners is the upsurge in the number of women, especially women in the managerial and professional ranks. According to the Women's Bureau of the U.S. Labor Department, 58 million women participated in the labor force (by working or looking for work) in 1992. That's impressive because as recently as 1975, only 34.5 million women—a 39% share—worked outside the home. Of the 54 million women employed during 1992, 40 million worked full-time and 14 million held part-time jobs. The Labor Department predicts that the number of working women will further rise to 71.4 million by 2005, a 47% share.

Number-crunching in *Megatrends 2000*, by John Naisbitt and Patricia Aburdene, reveals that "women without children are *more* likely to work than men. Today about 74% of men work. But 79% of women with no children under 18 work. So do 67% of women with children, almost as high a percentage as men. Half of women with small children work too."

By the numbers, women have nearly reached parity in the managerial ranks. Women occupy 14.7 million of the 31.2 million jobs the Labor Department labels "executive, administrative, and managerial," slightly ahead (47%) of their 45% representation in the general working population. Women actually outnumber men by 8.6 million to 7.8 million in the "professional specialty" category, which includes doctors, lawyers, nurses, teachers, scientists, and engineers.

Women holding executive-level jobs were still fairly scarce when I began my working career. American women moved into and up through the American workplace in three major waves that began in the early 1970s. According to *Success and Betrayal: The Crisis of Women in Corporate America,* by Sarah Hardesty and Nehama Jacobs, the first wave was the Vietnam war. "The selective service, with its loopholes and its capricious lottery system, forced younger men to defer their corporate dreams . . . Well-educated women rushed in to fill the vacuum of entry-level corporate vacancies."

The next wave came as a by-product of the civil rights movement of the '60s. The same spotlight that revealed the dearth of African-Americans in the office drew attention to other inequalities, notably women.

The third contributor to the "women's corporate awakening" was the debut in 1972 of *Ms* magazine and, eventually, a host of sister publications directed at executive women: *Working Woman,* (now defunct) *Savvy, Working Mother, Female Executive,* among others. "While relatively few women consciously identified with 'women's libbers,' unconsciously women all over American had internalized the message," write Hardesty and Jacobs. "Since there were few role models for women to follow, the best-educated, most information-hungry generation of women in history was prepared to read its way to the top."

They're still doing it. *Working Woman*'s 1992 circulation of 866,816 now exceeds that of *Fortune, Forbes, Nation's Business,* and every other business magazine except *Business Week.*

That women may have nearly achieved parity in workplace numbers and managerial jobs can be proven statistically. How well they've ascended to the ranks of top management depends on whom you listen to.

When the U.S. Labor Department reviewed 100 of the top *Fortune* 500 companies that did business with the federal government in 1991, it found that only 18% of officials and managers were female and that fewer than 7% of top managers were women. A 1993 study by Catalyst, a non-profit research organization, revealed that while the number of women who hold seats on *Fortune* 500 boards of directors has reached an all-time high of 721, this number represents only 6.2% of total board seats.

Most pessimistic of all is a 1991 report by the Feminist Majority Foundation which counted only 175 women among 6,502 corporate officers at the level of vice president or higher. At the current rate, the study concluded, women wouldn't shatter the glass ceiling to reach corporate equality with men for another *475 years!*

Fortunately, there's another side to the story. "If you look at the ranks of any major corporation below the top 20 people, you'll find that 50% of the next group of managers are women," says executive recruiter Lester Korn of Korn/Ferry International. Korn sees women making major breakthroughs into the corporate stratosphere between 1995 and 2000, after they've had 25 or 30 years of executive experience under their belts.

And there's more to executive life than the *Fortune* 500. An estimated five million women today run small- to medium-sized companies and, according to a recent study by Cognetics, Inc. and the Foundation for Women Business Owners, women-owned businesses surpass *Fortune* 500 corporations in the number of persons employed.

The future of women in the workplace looks even brighter. "Women may have missed out on the industrial age but they have already established themselves in the industries of the future," says *Megatrends 2000.* Industries of the future where women are prominent are finance, health care, computers, and science.

The presence of working women, many of them married and the mothers of babies and young children, has produced startling physical changes in the workplace. The U.S. Congress had to bend to changing gender demographics after the 1992 election brought 29 new women—24 in the House of Representatives, five in the Senate— and increased the female

Congressional population to a total of 55, twice as many as ever before. After the female senators pointed out that there was no ladies' room convenient to the Senate floor, a closet was quickly converted for that purpose. The Congress also had to quickly formulate a dress code to accommodate the bright new dresses and pants suits that now bring color to the formerly gray area.

Women in high office may be terrific role models, but the conspicuous presence of mothers in the today's workplace may be generating the bad manners of tomorrow. Following a speech I had given on manners in the workplace, a testy gentleman somewhat beyond middle age stood up to inquire, "Who taught you *your* manners?"

"My mother," I replied.

"Just what I figured," he said with a smug smirk. My mother had stayed home to teach *me* manners, but who taught my children their manners while I pursued a full-time career?

I believe that even with a very busy marriage and/or career, time can always be made to teach children the importance of manners. I have some doubt, however, that today's parents are in fact doing this. While I learned manners from my southern mother, today's children are learning their manners from the Killer B's: Beavis, Butt-head, and Bart. Also, I am not overly impressed with the progeny of the first wave of executive mothers who are now entering the work force. More on generation gap in manners in Chapter Four.

I have always held, with Florence Nightingale, that the woman who works beside men must expect no favors on account of her sex, and accept none.

—FANNY M. BAGBY (1884)

There seems to be a decided difference of opinion on how well men and women get along in the workplace. According to a Swain & Swain survey of *Fortune* 500 managers, 50% of the men believed they worked well with women but only 34% of the women believed the men worked well with them. Asked whether they accepted women as peers, 50% of the men said they did but only 33% of the women agreed.

Why the discrepancy? Partly because corporate America still is predominantly male in the upper management positions and it may be easier to "work well" with people you supervise than with those who supervise you. But another part of the discrepancy could result from the unrealistic expectations some women and men bring into the workplace.

Too often I have seen women, and sometimes men, who want to receive all the perks of top management without enduring all the hardships. Hardships include traveling on your own time, working regular 10-, 12-, and 14-hour days, and being on-call all the rest of time. The most important part of high-visibility, high-pay jobs that women and some men decline to perform is "cold-calling." Nobody *likes* cold calling, but in my view women lose a good share of corporate credibility when they try to avoid it.

I also think many women are wrong to try to be "one of the guys." I don't completely understand why, but some women seem to have a hard time coming back from lunch with a supervisor and separating a business-and-pleasure meal from the business-and-business work environment. Women who go out for after-work drinks with their supervisors are even more likely to get into ambiguous situations.

The question is not whether I treat you rudely, but whether you ever heard me treat anyone else better.

—HENRY HIGGINS IN *PYGMALION* BY GEORGE BERNARD SHAW

My approach to dealing with men and women in the office is a *slight* alteration on Professor Higgins'. I would treat men and women the same—not rudely but well. This policy applies on a grand level to hiring practices, job descriptions, and salaries. Just as importantly, it applies to day-to-day manners. Ladies, gentlemen, now hear this:

- ❖ When visitors enter your office, rise to greet them.
- ❖ Whoever reaches the door first shall open it and hold it open for those who follow. In case of a tie, let whoever totes the smaller load reach for the doorknob.
- ❖ If a co-worker is carrying a heavy package, offer to help.

❖ In elevators, he/she who is closest to the door shall be first to disembark.

❖ If a co-worker upsets a stack of papers, stop to help pick them up.

❖ If a co-worker or business guest needs help getting a coat on, lend a hand.

The rule? Respect the person, not the sex. The key to following the rule? Let these gestures come naturally, and for *everyone*.

One need only step into a modern office for a moment and glance around at the stenographers in their thin georgette blouses and high-heeled shoes, to realize how inappropriate gaudy, attractive clothes are in the business atmosphere . . . the business person who expects to have a worthy career, will find ostentation in clothes, and especially gaudy display, fatally detrimental to her ultimate success.

—LILLIAN EICHLER, *BOOK OF ETIQUETTE* (1923)

Too often in the office of the '90s—or, as we can see, in any decade since women joined the work force—women are consigned to subservient roles possibly because of the way they choose to dress. Enter any office and you see most men dressed in coats and tie ready for business, but you often can't tell whether the women are going to a cocktail party, a picnic, or a clean-up detail.

A woman who goes to work dressed as a Madonna wannabe in spiked heels, short skirts, tight pants, and low-cut blouses—or a woman clad in garish colors or trendy all black—should not be surprised if male and female co-workers don't take her as seriously as she thinks she should be.

Throughout my working career, I have been a strong advocate of the professional business suit for women—even when that suit was difficult to find in stores. That's not my idea, nor is it a particularly new one. Lillian Eichler's 1923 *Book of Etiquette* insisted that "the correctly tailored, neat business suit is indispensable—as any business woman will attest. There seems to be a dignity about a suit that is lacking in any other business gar-

A WOMAN WHO GOES TO WORK DRESSED AS A MADONNA WANNABE SHOULD NOT BE SURPRISED IF MALE AND FEMALE CO-WORKERS DON'T TAKE HER AS SERIOUSLY AS SHE THINKS SHE SHOULD BE.

ment." Eichler recommended smart English tweeds in heather, gray, or brown; jersey suits in dark colors and simple styles, and the then-popular navy blue serge suits. Plain white lawn or white batiste blouses were preferred complements.

Dress-for-success maven John T. Molloy endorses the business suit for women. His research shows that the "business uniform"—a skirted dark suit and contrasting blouse—"will give businesswomen a look of authority, which is precisely what they need."

Molloy found that it will also give them professional success. He asked managers to describe their female employees' style of dress and tracked their progress over the next three years. Molloy determined that female workers whose clothes were characterized as "extremely feminine" had lower salaries and were promoted less frequently. "The highest-paid women, on the other hand, were those whose dress was described as 'professional,' 'dull,' 'conservative,' 'non-sexy,' or 'non-frilly.'"

Some companies have written dress codes: suits (not jackets) and ties for men; suits and dresses (no pants suits) with hose for women. Most of the time, however, dress codes are a kind of corporate folklore, transmitted down the corporate hierarchy less by word-of-mouth than image-by-eye. Dress like the highest-ranking person of your sex in the company and you won't go *too* far wrong. Otherwise, acceptable business dress is mainly a matter of avoiding several common mistakes.

Seven Business Dress Don'ts for Men and Women

1. Don't wear the same suit/dress two days in a row.
2. Don't wear clothes that are too tight.
3. Don't wear boots to the office.
4. Don't wear flamboyant jewelry.
5. Don't go into your superior's office with your suit jacket off.
6. Don't go to work with your shoes unpolished.
7. Don't be daring.

Remember that as a teenager you are at the last stage in your life when you will be happy to hear that the phone is for you.

—FRAN LEBOWITZ, *SOCIAL STUDIES* (1977)

In addition to personnel affairs, the office of the '90s presents a number of technological challenges to civil behavior. Most of them have something to do with the telephone: placing calls, receiving calls, ducking calls. In Chapter 12, I'll take a stab at writing an etiquette book for the office of tomorrow. Here are a few tips on dealing with manners issues created by the telephonic technology of today.

Fax Machines

The fax machine is a wonderful invention that combines the speed of the telephone with the comprehensiveness of mail. Fax messages arrive as quickly as a telephone call, but the written form allows recipients to read them at *their* convenience. Fax machines are actually somewhat retro: they force people to actually *write*.

The fax is perfect for sending business correspondence, reports, press releases, promotional literature, or other communications for which time is of the essence. The fax is not appropriate in situations where thoughtfulness rather than time is of the essence. This would include invitations to business or social events, thank-you notes, letters of condolence, and other types of highly personal correspondence.

Don't use the office fax for trivial pursuits, whether it's your dynamite chili recipe, a clipping about your ex-boss' money-laundering conviction, or the day's eerily prescient *Far Side* cartoon. Never fax anything the least bit confidential: one never knows whose eyes might fall on the transmission before the intended recipient collects it.

Always call the recipient before tying up the line with a lengthy fax, say five pages or more. He or she may prefer that you send it by mail. Remember that unless it is plain paper, machine fax paper fades. If you don't know what kind of equipment your recipient has, send a fax in advance for speed and if the document needs to be saved, also mail an original.

Voicemail

Voicemail, the industrial-strength version of the home answering machine, is in some respects a very good thing. It removes the risk that a secretary will mangle an incoming message or lose the pink memo slip. But the voicemail sounds cold (and it's worse when it tries to sound friendly), it's subject to malfunction, it seldom permits the caller to obtain information as to the party's whereabouts, and it can definitely provoke uncivil behavior.

Screening calls is not inherently rude. You are no more obliged to accept all phone calls than you are to write thank-you notes for junk mail. When leaving a voicemail message, you need not account for your absence, but you should specify exactly what information you wish the caller to provide. Usually this is limited to name and number, time of call, reason for call. Most voicemail users want brief messages explaining the reason for the call, but I've noticed an increasing number users request *detailed* messages. You might also offer callers some course of action to take—a home phone number or a colleague's extension—if their business is urgent and how they might reach a "live" human voice.

What is not up to you is what I consider the number-one (and really only) rule of voicemail: He/she who accepts voicemail messages *must* return the call. Certainly, all of us can recall innumerable instances when our voicemail messages were not returned. I would label them innumerable instances of atrocious business manners and give great thought to how badly I needed to work with those individual's companies.

Voicemail callers need to be concise but thorough. State who you're calling (in case of a mishap); who *you* are (including affiliation and title if you are unknown to the voicemail user); date and time; brief message; and your phone number (even if you know they know it).

Since voicemail systems and answer systems are forms of community property, don't say anything you don't want everybody else in the company to hear. If your calling itself may be problematic, don't leave any message.

Lastly, don't rush your message. Most modern systems are voice-activated, which means that they'll keep recording as long as you keep talking.

Portable Phones

Portable phones are everywhere—on planes and trains, in restaurants and hotel lobbies, on the street, in theaters. Granting people capability of doing business virtually everywhere gives them another way to behave uncivilly virtually everywhere.

The main rule for using portable phones: don't raise your voice. It's bad manners because it annoys everyone around you, and it's bad business to broadcast your activities to everyone within earshot. Because of their ever-tightening seating arrangements, airplane phones are the worst producers of passive noise pollution.

Don't take your portable phone out to lunch; don't invite it to parties. Unless you're a physician or otherwise involved in life-or-death missions, you probably don't need to take your phone into theaters, libraries, other people's offices, or any setting where silence is golden. Moveover, watch what you say: portable phones use radio lines that can be picked up by anything that uses the air waves, from other cellular phones to CBs to home baby monitors.

HUMAN BEINGS FIRST, MEN AND WOMEN SECOND

Miscommunication as the Root of All Gender-Benders

"Profane, foul or discourteous language over the telephone is debarred by the rules of telephone etiquette. Some states impose a heavy fine for such a breach of etiquette."

GOOD FORM AND SOCIAL ETHICS
Fannie Dickerson Chase, 1913.

The point is that, for good and ill, there are profound differences in the ways women and men approach and solve problems. Women cooperate and men negotiate.

—ANN W. RICHARDS, GOVERNOR OF TEXAS (1993)

If a man mulls over a decision, they say, "He's weighing the options." If a woman does it, they say, "She can't make up her mind."

—BARBARA PROCTOR (1975)

The title of this chapter is a quotation by none other than my husband, Gordon. It is a principle I subscribe to wholeheartedly and always try to live by. So does he.

Work for men is easier in some ways because they are not normally expected to stay home and tend to the children—not in today's world and certainly not in the era when I was raising children. Also, it used to be normal for men to pursue the dominant career, to earn the larger income, and to be involved in the career with the most promotion potential. It was not in the least "normal" for a man to move to further his wife's career.

But Gordon did it.

A newspaper wrote a story about us the first time Gordon moved with me. The reporter said, "I can't believe you're following her to Minnesota!" Gordon said, "I'm not *following* her anywhere: I'm going *with* her."

The altered attitude toward women in the workplace, particularly executive-level women, is not always reflected in the language used to describe them and what they do. The human-beings-first philosophy is constantly undermined by the brazen discrimination applied to descriptions of similar workplace behavior as performed by women and men. Workplace sociologists and authorities on language call it a double standard when:

❖ A businessman is aggressive; a businesswoman is pushy.

❖ He is attentive to detail; she is picky.

❖ He speaks his mind; she is opinionated.

❖ He exercises authority; she's a bitch.

Of course, like most double standards, this male/female dichotomy can be a two-edged sword.

❖ A businesswoman is sensitive; a businessman is soft.

❖ She is prudent; he is gutless (or worse!).

❖ She is cooperative; he is passive.

❖ She knows when to compromise; he lacks principles.

❖ She is charming; he is effeminate.

Beyond stereotypical labels, some evidence exists that women and men really do communicate differently in the work environment. The female style of communication is often very different from men's, and sometimes that hurts them in business. For one thing, women hedge. Where a man will enthusiastically put forth a proposal—"I've got a great idea . . ."—a woman will often couch her solution in qualifiers—"Here's something that might work . . ."

I've also noticed that women, much more than men, perhaps inadvertently add 'isn't it?' or 'shouldn't we?' or 'don't you think?' to the end of sentences. When women say these things, they intend to invite feedback and participation. Unfortunately, men misread the questions as uncertainty and approval seeking.

There is also a male/female breakdown on the listening end of communication. Women typically look steadily at a speaker, nod, and make regular *mmm-hmm* sounds to signal reception. Men typically make sporadic eye contact, nod infrequently or not all, maybe play with something with their hands, or wander around the room. Believe it or not, they may still be listening closely and taking in everything you say.

Scientific evidence exists to indicate that the male communication style—assertiveness and the seeming life-threatening allergy to asking directions or for most other forms of advice—is subtly sanctioned by society. Communications professors Gerri Smith of California State University-Sacramento and Sue DeWine of Ohio University videotaped male and female actors portraying employees asking their superiors for help. They had 140 real supervisors watch the tapes and rate competence levels.

Women who asked questions received positive ratings. Men who asked the same questions were rated negatively. The study concluded that supervisors equate competence in males with independence, and competence in women with seeking assistance. "We continue to expect women to seek help, while we expect men to solve their own problems."

Miscommunication is acknowledged as a serious problem in the business world. Management guru Peter Drucker estimates that 60% of management problems stem from faulty communication. The late Supreme Court Justice Louis D. Brandeis contended that "nine-tenths of the serious controversies which arise in life result from misunderstanding."

A 1993 *McCall's* magazine survey went so far as to quantify the male/female miscommunication gap: 61% of the women polled say men don't know what women want; 62% of the women say that men will *never* understand them.

A root cause of miscommunication lies in the very words we use—and forces are at play to control them. The *Los Angeles Times* has issued a 19-page pamphlet entitled "Guidelines on Ethnic, Racial, Sexual, and Other Identification," listing words and phrases that may not appear in the pages of the *Times* and why these terms are offensive. *Mailman* is out because "many women hold this job." *Co-ed* is "considered offensive to female college students." *Man-made* must be replaced by "artificial, manufactured, or synthetic." Other banned-in-L.A. terms include *bra-burner, crazy, divorcee, ghetto, hick, hillbilly, holy rollers, Indians,* and *white trash. L.A. Times* reporters dare not even describe someone as *normal.*

The newspaper might have gone off the deep end, but a strategic dose of *voluntary* language control can go a long way to curtailing office gender-benders. Since the moment larger numbers of women began migrating up from the secretarial pool, men have used superficially friendly, flattering, seemingly harmless sexist terms to keep them in their place. Sometimes these terms are meant to hurt, sometimes not, mostly the men have done it out of habit.

Men plead consternation with rules that seem constantly in flux. They *intend* no offense, and therefore take umbrage when offense is taken. Let's give them the benefit of very little doubt and assume that it's just a matter of education. Gentlemen, take notes. There will be a quiz.

MEN PLEAD CONSTERNATION WITH RULES THAT SEEM CONSTANTLY IN FLUX. THEY INTEND NO OFFENSE, AND THEREFORE TAKE UMBRAGE WHEN OFFENSE IS TAKEN.

10 Words and Phrases Not To Utter At Work

1. Girl
2. Gal
3. Baby/babe
4. Sweetheart/sweetie
5. Honey
6. Darling/Dear
7. Bimbo
8. Chick
9. Broad
10. *Any* colloquial term for breasts

I have not listed several far more inflammatory terms because (it is hoped) my readers would not dream of using them in an office or anywhere. The terms on the list are those that might be considered quite suitable and proper in other contexts; perhaps they have alternative meanings. But things being as they are, they do not belong in the workplace.

Don't use them toward a woman you are addressing and don't use them to refer to a woman who is not present. Think of them as sexual equivalents of ethnic slurs and don't use them at all.

Where, in the spirit of fair play, is my list of ten words women must not say to or about men? Sorry, I can't think of any. Culturally, there's nothing degrading about *being* a man or any quality of maleness. Call a man one of the many synonyms for a part of the male anatomy and Average Joe turns into Rhett Butler: Frankly, my dears, he doesn't give a damn.

There is one perpetual law running through all our intercourse with others . . . This law is recognized in the commercial, and it should be strictly observed in the etiquette of social life. In short, in the many varied amenities of life, the fundamental rule of action should be the golden rule: "To do unto others as we would that others should do unto us."

—HILL'S MANUAL (1878)

What's the rule for dealing with miscommunication in the workplace? The golden one will do for starters. Treat everyone with the quintessential formula for civility described in the Bible: "Do unto others as you would have them do unto you."

The only differences that matter are differences between individuals. Everybody is the same in one sense: they are all special and unique. Discrimination and harassment, sexual or otherwise, have no place in the workplace. Individual responsibility and morality do.

One way to self-enforce the golden rule is through constant communication. If you're a manager, you should keep employees totally informed of any and all changes that will affect them—you'd want your superiors to do the same for you, wouldn't you? If people don't know what's going on, they always assume the worst. Morale collapses, productivity suffers. I always tell everyone about upcoming changes as soon as I know about them. In doing so, I make sure I explain their roles or possible roles in the new set-up.

How can you open up lines of communication with your staff? Two suggestions:

❖ Don't use secretaries and assistants as buffers.

❖ Arrange to have some form of personal contact with all of your people at least once every day.

The Golden Rule is a fine starting point, but you won't get far without first-rate business communication skills. The first communication task to master is the delicate art of the introduction, an elementary activity that makes many businesspeople feel verbally challenged.

In terms of self-introductions, keep it as simple as possible: first name, last name, title. "I'm Beverly Patrick, president of Professional Risk Management Services." If you prefer to be called by a nickname that differs from the formal name on your business card or resume—"Bill" for "William," "Kathy" for "Katherine"—introduce yourself with the nickname or say, "I'm Margaret Smith but you can call me 'Maggie.'" However, *never* presume to nickname those who introduce themselves with their complete names. If a gentleman introduces himself as Archibald, it is not your privilege to call him Archie.

During the brief course of the introduction, look your new acquaintance right in the eye and offer a firm, confident handshake.

The protocol for introducing other people to each other hasn't changed much over the course of a century. Introduce less eminent to more eminent. You wish to "make someone acquainted with someone" or you "would like someone to meet someone." The person of lower status plays the active role: he or she does the meeting. The person of higher status plays the passive role: he or she is being met.

Determining who's on top is obviously a judgment call subject to a multitude of *faux pas*, but Letitia Baldridge provides helpful guidelines. Introduce:

❖ A younger person *to* an older person

❖ A peer in your company *to* a peer in another company

❖ A junior executive *to* a senior executive

❖ A fellow executive *to* a customer or client

No act in all of management—save that of thinking itself—is given as much time as the spoken word. Yet no other act in all of management is as grossly underutilized as this one in which one executive speaks to another.

—ALLAN COX, *THE MAKING OF THE ACHIEVER*

Once the introductions are out of the way, there are plenty of ways to foster clear lines of business communication:

- ❖ *Avoid profanity or obscenity.* It offends people and bespeaks a deficient imagination or vocabulary. I know it's unfair, but foul language is often more offensive coming from a woman.

- ❖ *Use proper English and correct grammar.* Don't say "ain't." Enunciate the "g" at the end of words like "somethin'" and "nothin.'" And like punctuating all your verbalized clauses with "like" makes you sound like an idiot.

- ❖ *Grow your vocabulary.* You don't have to sound as if you are William F. Buckley, but a few strategically dropped, properly used three-syllable-plus words will never fail to impress.

- ❖ *Avoid techtalk.* Don't show off by using technical terms—of your industry or of your sub-specialty within the industry—unless you know everyone present understands them. The purpose of conversation is to communicate, not to exclude.

- ❖ *Eschew psychobabble.* Expounding on the feral impulses of your inner child may work in California therapy groups, but it doesn't belong in offices—even California offices.

- ❖ *Watch your body language.* Some men and women have a tendency to undermine their words by slumping in chairs, cocking their heads, and otherwise signaling that they need not be taken seriously.

- ❖ *Learn how to listen.* Keep your eyes on the speaker and your mouth closed until the speaker has finished saying his or her piece.

- ❖ *Consider voice and speech training.* A little professional help, available in all major cities, can go a long way toward putting a polished shine on your business communication skills.

What Women Should *Never* Do In The Office

CRY

Men hate it, think it's unfair, manipulative, taking advantage of their sex. Other women in the office hate it even more for much the same reasons. Women who cry in the office for any reason seem weak, out of control, totally unprofessional, unable to handle the job. Nothing fouls up male/female lines of communication worse than crying. Men use crying to justify every rotten thing they've ever done to women: "One word and she turns on the waterworks!" Get mad, walk away, barricade yourself in your office—but don't let them see you cry.

What Men Should *Never* Do In The Office

SHOUT

The objections to shouting for men are pretty much the same as the ones against crying for women: it's unfair, it's manipulative, the implied physical threat takes unfair advantage of his sex, it's totally unprofessional. A man who shouts to seize control relinquishes any hope of getting it. As with crying, shouting ruptures lines of communication. "Every time I open my mouth, he blows his top." There's no room for it in today's office.

Evil communications corrupt good manners.

—I CORINTHIANS 15:33

Many of the impediments to human-beings-first result from communication barriers, ample long-standing barriers, but none too high to be surmounted by the indomitable power of good manners. I know because crossed wires caused a terrific collision in my own company—right before my eyes, in fact—between two senior people who had previously worked together amicably for years.

"Sally," in her late 30s, is a member of my senior staff. "Charlie" is a senior vice president who works for one of our main customers. Charlie, in his late 50s, is "old school" (or at least from an older school than I). Most women and some men view Charlie as a well-intentioned, basically likable, unregenerate male chauvinist. Sally had long been annoyed by Charlie's old-time manners and paternalism, but somehow they managed—in the silently suffering style of a cat and dog forced to live in the same home—to work together.

Until the day the dam burst.

It happened during a meeting when we took up a technical insurance point. Charlie turned to Sally and said, "Let me explain that you."

Sally snapped, "I know that just as well as you do, you jerk!"

I thought that was it, but after the meeting Sally caught Charlie in the hall and told him what she *really* thought about him.

How did Charlie respond? He apologized. "Sally, it was a completely stupid remark. I didn't mean it. I shouldn't have said it. We all know you know your stuff."

What did Sally do? She spit it back in his face. "Oh, please," she sneered, "Now you really insult my intelligence. Just who do you think you're fooling? Everyone in this office knows how you are."

Who's at fault? Obviously both of them. But let's step back from the sexual communication barrier and see how manners might have helped avoid this disaster.

Charlie suffers from the very common condition—a very common American condition—of confusing social manners and business manners. Many people cannot distinguish their business lives from their social lives, a blurring of boundaries that leads to the workplace delusion that we're all friends. How many times have you heard someone say, "At the XYZ Corporation we're all just *one big happy family*." Right—and they probably fight like one, too.

The colleagues-as-family fallacy (which I address at greater length in Chapter 7) is certainly one source of Charlie-Sally friction. If Charlie views himself as the benevolent father, Sally must be the wayward daughter. The sitcom conclusion: "Father Knows Best" turns into "Married With Children."

Sally's problem is the sequoia-sized chip on her shoulder that automatically evokes massive retaliation for the slightest of slights, real or imagined. But does the severity of Sally's retribution punishment fit the severity of Charlie's crime? Does her flagrant overreaction demonstrate strength or weakness?

The answer lies in one of the underlying principals of good manners. Manners are not about suffering fools in silence, nor are they about enduring cruel slights. There is nothing "polite" about passively suffering belittling comments, errors, or cruel jokes at your expense. Indeed, a mastery of manners and the art of the subtle response has about it the delicate air of the martial arts. Kung Fu masters don't flail around making vain threats. Neither do workplace manners masters. The point is knowing just how far to go make your point—and nip a potential problem in the bud.

The typical mistake—Sally's mistake—is to suffer in silence too long, let the pressure build, and then blow your stack. The office "sniper" belittles your competence. You shrug it off the first time it happens. Then you shrug it off again. Finally you must confront the lout: "Excuse me, do you have a problem with my work? If so, let's discuss it. If not—or if you're just nervous about the new account—then why not find a more constructive outlet?" That should do it. Few snipers can bear face-to-face contact.

What does the doctrine of good manners mandate to Sally: Correct the error in a firm, good-natured way—and then, for heaven's sake, move on.

Sally blew it. By overreacting she turns Charlie into an object of sympathy. Worse yet, she plays into the stereotype many women are struggling to break. Sally and I talked at length about the incident and came to the conclusion that we all need to listen less to the *words* of what's being said and more to the *music.* When we listen to the melody, we are less likely to take offense. (Whoever heard of "fighting melodies"?) We need to remember that just because we don't like to hear something, it is not necessarily intended to put us down.

In truth, both sides deserve plenty of blame for instigating workplace miscommunication between the sexes. Women often metaphorically shoot themselves in the foot when by taking things that are said to them—by men or by other women—personally. Too often women are offended by loud voices and harsh intonations. Business is stressful and often as not the tone of a voice is an expression of that stress. It is not necessarily a sign of anger or disapproval, and it is not meant to offend.

Positive behavior can be equally misleading. Speaking pleasantly doesn't necessarily mean someone is pleased with you. (Are you always pleased with the people you speak pleasantly to?) Perhaps they just want to be polite—just like you.

I have found that some people have a very difficult time separating personal feelings from professional discussions. Everyone has to learn that, after a heated discussion at a conference table or in an office, you must get up and go forward as business associates and not as enemies. You should not take it personally.

That's the key: Human beings first. Men and women second. Professionals always.

THE HIT PARADE MEETS
WOODSTOCK MEETS MTV

Forging a Corporate Merger of the Generations

The old believe everything; the middle-aged suspect everything; the young know everything.

—Oscar Wilde (1894)

There is a truism about manners that can be stated didactically: Each generation believes that the manners of the generation that follows it have gone to hell in a hand basket.

—Russell Lynes, *Architectural Digest* (1986)

O ne factor that compounds male-female workplace conflicts is the spontaneous conflict between the generations. Just as today's workplace is forcing the two sexes to learn work together, it is also forging working relationships between three very different generations with very different sets of work habits and values.

Generation One is my generation, people born during the Depression and World War II who are now between 50 and 60. *Generation Two* are the fabled postwar Baby Boomers, now in their late 30s and early 40s. *Generation Three*, the so-called Baby Busters, are the 20/30-somethings.

There is one more generation, the *G.I. Generation*, of people born from the beginning of the century to the mid-1920s. Most of them, however, are retired or have ascended to a management strata far removed from generational ground wars.

Some of the generational hostility is deeper and hotter than the conflicts between the sexes. And the differences are not caused by divergent communication styles and crossed wires so much as by profoundly different value systems and disagreement over the very meaning of life.

All these were honored in their generations, and were the glory of their times.

—Ecclesiastes 30:24

Generation One, often called the Silent Generation, didn't learn their manners from etiquette books. They had their manners drilled into them by parents, by teachers, by the entire community, even by the media—the

Question: Why do you want to work for the XYZ Corporation?

GENERATION ONE

I WOULD LIKE THE OPPORTUNITY TO WORK HERE BECAUSE I AM SO MOTIVATED BY THE CHALLENGE AND THE POTENTIAL FOR CAREER ADVANCEMENT. I KNOW THAT WITH SOME HOURS AND A LITTLE "ELBOW GREASE," I CAN TURN THOSE SALES FIGURES AROUND!

books, magazines, radio programs, and movies of the day. Wherever we turned we received instructions detailing *exactly* what was expected of us. When we faltered, our parents or any passing stranger was likely to set us straight.

What were the rules? According to Letitia Baldridge, until the 1970s a "polite" man was obliged to perform the following services for all women he respected:

- ❖ Hold doors open for her
- ❖ Hold her coat for her
- ❖ Light her cigarettes
- ❖ Never allow her to carry a package
- ❖ Walk curbside with her, to protect her from being splashed by passing vehicles (originally buggies)
- ❖ Run around to open her car door
- ❖ Push in her chair at the table

❖ Never shake her hand unless she offered it first

❖ Jump up and remain standing for her until she sat down

❖ Refrain from discussing such subjects as business, because she probably wouldn't understand

What rules govern behavior today? The men of this generation wish they knew! Here's the kind of situation men of Generation One persistently encounter:

A very good male friend of mine was in a parking garage. When he got to the door of the elevator lobby, he noticed a woman with an armful of packages hurrying across the lot. He waited at the door to the building and held the door open for her. When she got there, she turned to him and snapped, "You didn't have to wait and hold the door for me. I'm perfectly capable of doing it myself."

He was really confused and later said to me, "Women! I just don't know how to deal with them any more."

Men of Generation One were conditioned to *always* pay the dinner check. In today's business world, however, men are regularly invited to lunch and other business meals by women—women of their own and younger generations—who fully expect to pay. When the two value systems go head-to-head, conflicts erupt. Is there anything more absurd and embarrassing than two professionals fighting to *pay* a check? And what are they fighting about? Of course they're fighting over the true currency of the workplace: power and priority.

Not surprisingly, common sense—and common decency—turn out to be the best way to quell generational/gender warfare. In *Business Protocol*, Jan Yager writes, "Having a door opened for a woman by man may still be polite in almost all corporate or company settings, but having a man pick up a tab . . . has become a less universal occurrence . . . The person of higher status or who initiated the meeting will most likely pick up the check." (Much more on the etiquette of business meals in Chapter 8.)

❧❦❧

Generation Two are the Baby Boomers, now 76 million strong. Like previous generations, their parents and the media taught them good manners and for awhile they were all right. Then came the '60s—long hair on men, love beads, bra burning, marijuana—and manners went up in smoke.

Now the Baby Boomers have cut their hair, purchased suits and bras, and comprise about half the amorphous category known as "boss." But the subject of manners still seems faintly musty and embarrassing. This was the generation of sex, drugs, and rock-and-roll, the generation that shunned Wall Street in favor of Woodstock. Despite the camouflage of power suits and straight jobs, Boomers still insist it's what's *inside* you that really matters. It's a generation in which what you see is not necessarily what you get.

I find Generation Two the most difficult generation to deal with, perhaps because there seem to be more of them in the workplace now than anyone else. Women of this age group tend to pay more attention to innuendo. They appear to more quickly take offense at apprehended slights and take issue with particular words and phrases. Generation Two women seem to be especially intolerant of Generation One men.

Question: Why do you want to work for the XYZ Corporation?

GENERATION TWO

I WANT TO WORK FOR XYZ BECAUSE I TOTALLY SUPPORT THE COMPANY'S POSITION ON PRESERVING THE ENVIRONMENT. ALSO, THERE ISN'T A GLASS CEILING HERE. I AM ESPECIALLY EXCITED BY THE INTERNAL TASK FORCE ON PROMOTING WOMEN. THE ON-SITE DAY CARE IS ALSO APPEALING.

I recall an incident when I traveled with some male and female colleagues by van to a meeting away from the office. One of the Generation Two women in the group was really ragging one of the older men who was unloading our supplies from the van. Finally, he snapped and said, "Hold your horses, little girl!"

"Don't you *ever* call me little girl," she fired back.

Most probably, had another man been harassing him, he would have said to him, "Hold your horses, little *boy*!" But she seemed anxious to take offense because it was coming from an older male.

It could be that Generation One men have trouble with Generation Two women because the men tend to confuse business manners with social manners. Women who bristle when complimented on their appearance, resist being ushered through doorways, or refuse to allow men to pay their expenses may *appear* to be condemning the concept of manners. Absolutely not! Their complaint is not about having manners in the office, but with men who use social manners in the office toward women and business manners toward other men. Social manners for some and business manners for others implies that serious discussions must be suspended when women are around. Men may do this in the spirit of helpfulness, but it is not at all helpful to their female colleagues or to anyone else.

None of this would happen if everyone were able to overlook gender in the workplace—remember, human beings first, men and women second? Unfortunately, no generation is even close to managing that.

❧❧❧

For Generation Three, manners are something of an unsolved mystery. But even finding the right label for those born during the '60 and '70s is something of a mystery.

You hear them called Baby Busters a lot, probably because it sounds cute after Baby Boomers. But it's dead wrong. The early 1960s produced one of the biggest birth spurts in U.S. history and there are now even more Busters—80 million—than Boomers. Other suggested appellations include "Generation X" or "Xers," "Slackers," "Twentynothings," and "Postics" (as in post-Yuppies).

Whatever we choose to call them, I've seen many talented Generation Three junior executives—men and women—whose social rough edges have become a real brake on their careers. A subset of the problem is their poor grammar, both in written and oral communication. It's really difficult when people don't know what the rules are and have to ask "where they're at." Boy, you've really said a mouthful. It takes more than dress-for-success seminars or scratch golf scores to overcome these problems.

Generation Three is the most self-centered Me Generation yet, a generation of individuals exclusively concerned with themselves. For example, a young graduate from a major college who was working at my company stated that employers were legally required to give vacations. This kind of person is too wrapped up in "Me" to even think about what he or she is saying.

Question: Why do you want to work for the XYZ Corporation?

XYZ
CORPORATION
Personnel
Dept.

GENERATION THREE

THIS COMPANY WOULD BE A GOOD PLACE FOR ME BECAUSE THE HOURS AREN'T TOO LONG . . . I COULD STILL HAVE A PERSONAL LIFE. THE MONEY IS GREAT. THE ANNUAL LEAVE BENEFIT IS SUPER. AND THE WORK DOESN'T SEEM TOO HARD!

This is a generation of people who, when someone says "God bless you" after a sneeze, are likely to snap, "I don't believe in God." This is a generation that instead of considering the source, say, "To heck with it, I won't be bothered."

Many executives these days have trouble coping with Generation Three. They have been called the most difficult generation ever to manage because the traditional motivations—money and prestige—have little appeal. They want to put in their time, get home, and get on with their "real" life.

Generation Three appears to lack motivation for climbing the ladder of success. A Roper Poll found that only 26% of people in their 20s wanted to be boss. Half the respondents to a *USA Today*/CNN survey of 18–29 year-olds viewed their jobs as simply what they do for a living: only 40% of Baby Boomers and 26% of people over 50 felt the same way.

There is evidence that Generation Three even speaks a different language than the rest of us. The Irish-Canadian-Valley Girl intonation? The one that turn statements into questions? Linguist Cynthia McLemore calls it "uptalk" and finds it prevalent among Baby Busters all over the country. "I'm going to lunch?" "I'm having a meeting in my office?" "I'm your new assistant?" That's what she's talking about. To many of us, uptalk communicates Generation Three's uncertainty and lack of direction, but it doesn't make them any easier to manage.

In their defense, Generation Three's bad manners, self-absorption, and diminished language skills can be explained—if not excused—by poor economic prospects and absentee parenting. Nearly 40% of Generation Three are children of divorce. For those families that remained intact, the job commitments of two-income families turned many into "latchkey children" who returned home to empty houses and watched, according to *USA Today*, "an average of 33,000 murders on TV and in the movies by age 16."

Still, it's much too early to give up hope and I'm sure they will come up with much to offer the rest of us. If nothing else, they have street sense and a strong instinct for survival from which we can learn.

⚜

A black hole of established behavioral codes involves working for a female boss. It's a situation that the three generations adapt to in very different ways.

Generation One began its working life when female superiors were few and far between. Generation Two women *are* the bosses of today. Generation Three (as statistics cited in Chapter Two indicate) are encountering a working world in which they are far more likely to have a female supervisor than any previous generation.

Generational differences can be further broken down into two subsets: women managing men and women managing women.

In *Upward Mobility*, Owen Edwards points out that it is hardly unprecedented for women to manage men. "Men have always worked for women. Where men once did the bidding of Queen Elizabeth I or rallied to the command of Jeanne d'Arc, they work now for just plain Liz and Joan. . . . And though in the best of all possible business worlds, no adjustments would have to be made and transitions would demand nothing more than substituting 'Ms.' for 'Mr.,' such is rarely the case."

Men of Generation One, raised to hold coats, push in chairs, and never broach the dreary subject of business when ladies are present, must drastically alter their business manners when the lady is the boss. But younger males accustomed to equitable relations with female co-workers also have problems.

Some of the blame can be attributed to elementary biology. Some men can't believe that *any* woman who spends much time with them—including or maybe especially the boss—would fail to be interested in them as men. The easy banter and borderline flirting that often accompany close workplace relationships heighten the sexual tension.

There's also conditioning, the residue of innumerable books, movies, and TV shows that depict man as boss and woman as underling. Despite the very best intentions to celebrate the brave new world of workplace equality, men subconsciously feel that working for a woman violates the old world order. Think about it: How many men of *any* generation are truly comfortable when a woman is behind the wheel of a car? My guess is about the same percentage as feel truly comfortable with a woman in the driver's seat at work.

For men of all generations working for women, it's time to establish a few ground rules to eliminate or at least minimize conflict or embarrassment. The *Complete Office Handbook*, by Mary A. DeVries, offers the following guidelines to men with a lady boss:

- ❖ Treat her with the same respect you would grant a male executive.
- ❖ Let your boss indicate whether your relationship will be formal or informal.

❖ Allow your boss to set the time and place for work-related duties.

❖ Do not misinterpret her friendliness as a romantic overture.

How do women feel about working for female bosses? A 1993 survey by *Working Woman* determined that, in a reversal of a decades-old trend, the majority of the respondents did *not* prefer male bosses. Over 60% said the supervisor's gender didn't matter and 17% preferred a female.

The *Working Woman* survey is less definitive as to whether women feel women bosses bear a "special responsibility" to other women employees. Only 54% said women bosses have a special responsibility, while 50% said women managers should do what's best for the company *without making a point of speaking out for women.* Feelings on this point break down along generational lines: 61% of women 40 and older believe women have a responsibility to other women, while only 45% of those under agree.

Eighty-five percent of the respondents had had women bosses and the experience had made only a third of them more negative about the experience. *Biggest advantages:* women bosses are more sensitive about work/family issues (41%). *Biggest gripes:* women bosses are tougher on female employees (34%); women bosses are picky (38%); women bosses are exclusively concerned with their own careers (32%).

Whether she is a typist or manager of a great concern, the ideal business woman is accurate, orderly, quick, and impersonal. By "impersonal" is meant exactly that! Her point of view must be focused on the work in hand not on her own reactions to it, or to any one's reactions to herself.

—EMILY POST, *ETIQUETTE* (1937)

Problems arise between female managers and female subordinates because the two are the same but not equal. Female secretaries tend to see their bosses as older girl friends or surrogate big sisters—which obviously wouldn't happen with male bosses. Rapport crumbles when boss tells female assistant to retype a letter or fetch some coffee.

The first rule of female manager/female subordinate business etiquette: Don't let the sex of your boss or employee mislead you into sharing intimate details of your personal life. Inevitably, that confession or confidence will come back to haunt you, at best only embarrassing you and at the worst harming your career.

The best way for female employees to deal with female managers of any generation? Treat your boss according to the rules of etiquette appropriate to her status, not her gender. Take a look at how people in the company behave toward men and other women of comparable status in the firm and treat your female boss accordingly. Don't harbor fantasies for intimacy with your female boss, and don't expect her to carry the banner for your "cause."

The *Working Women* survey concludes, bittersweetly, that "women still expect female bosses to set a good example and help other women, but they don't expect them to take on the whole cause, particularly if the career cost is high . . . But the majority—61%—have seen enough good and bad bosses to understand that gender isn't necessarily a guide to a good manager. And that constitutes progress."

HAVE JOB, WILL TRAVEL

Rules of the Road—1990s Edition

*"The first rule of precedence to remember is
'Ladies first.' There are only a few exceptions
to this rule, as we shall presently see."*

THE NEW BOOK OF ETIQUETTE

Lillian Eichler, 1924.

The three things that distinguish an experienced woman traveler are courtesy, poise, and a regard for the rights of others.
—LILLIAN EICHLER, *NEW BOOK OF ETIQUETTE* (1934)

There's no reason to behave any differently from normal when you travel. In fact, there's no reason to behave at all. You're never going to see these people again, so what do you care?
—P.J. O'ROURKE, *MODERN MANNERS: AN ETIQUETTE BOOK FOR RUDE PEOPLE* (1989)

raveling for business is a necessary evil in the '90s. Few of us really like to travel on business. At its rare best, a business trip can be a welcome break from the humdrum routine of the office. At its usual worst, it is an exercise in frustration, discomfort, tedium, and fatigue that makes the humdrum routine of the office feel like a day at the beach.

For better or worse, women have in the '90s become full partners in the agony of business travel. According to the U.S. Travel Data Center, women comprise 40% of all business travelers. Radisson Hotels reports that 44% of its guests are female, up from under 30% only eight years ago.

To accommodate the woman business traveler, hotels have done everything from creating special high-security wings to making sure all rooms are equipped with hair-dryers and skirt hangers. Restaurants accommodate women dining solo with small tables equipped with reading lamps and formulate special menus of lighter fare aimed at women. Airport gift shops are stocking more stockings and other women's personal effects. Even airport cocktail lounges are making conscious efforts to clean up their acts.

It was not ever thus.

It was not *that* many years ago that women were not allowed to travel on business, particularly with a male colleague. There is a major railroad in Richmond, Virginia, my home town, that would hire male secretaries to travel with male executives.

For the most part, that has changed—but it didn't change altogether overnight. In traveling for business over the years, I have endured—and enjoyed—a fair share of gender-related mishaps. I have been checked into rooms that were already occupied and have had people attempt to check into my room while I was occupying it. Male colleagues have assumed that they could have adjoining rooms to mine—and made sure I knew they left the middle door unlocked.

One night in the Whistle Stop Bar at the very proper Hotel Roanoke I was having what I thought was a very professional discussion with a gentleman who, in the course of the conversation, told me that he had been married for 42 years. I was astonished to find out that he had taken me for a hooker "plying my trade," as he later informed me. This may be less surprising if you know that at this time, in Roanoke, there were still restaurants that women were not even allowed to enter, sit down, and eat in.

Health clubs, 24-hour room service, HBO; try as they might, no one can disguise the dislocation of today's business travel. Women, though, encounter special problems.

Security is one of the problems, and hotels and motels are tackling it. The use of electronic key-cards helps keep room keys out of the wrong hands. Hotels have installed double and triple locks on room doors and have upgraded the lighting in hallways and parking areas.

The Ritz-Carlton Hotel in Chicago, for example, assigns female guests to special rooms in the north end of the hotel. Security guards stationed on guest elevators overnight make sure that everyone who enters has a room key. The Loews L'Enfant Plaza in Washington has male staff members escort unaccompanied female guests to their cars in the hotel parking garage.

There are plenty of things women can do to protect themselves. When checking in, they can register with only a first initial and last name. If the desk clerk calls out your room number to the bellman, quietly request another room, one whose number hasn't been announced to everybody within shouting distance.

Let a bellman or a male companion accompany you to your room and check the bathroom, closets, and under the bed for intruders. Some women refuse to admit room-service until the receipt is slipped under the door.

An irksome problem, especially for women, is dealing with unwanted attention from people they encounter in the course of their journey. It begins on the plane or train when a seatmate strikes up a conversation and you would prefer to work/read/sleep—anything but get chatty with a stranger. If vague, noncommittal responses to initial conversation gambits fail to deter, a polite explanation that you must work/read/sleep works on all but the most persistent. No, it is not rude for someone to try to hold a conversation with you on a plane or train. Neither is it rude for you to politely decline to have one.

Other challenges to a woman traveler's privacy occur in hotels, bars, and restaurants. Proper dress is one way to deter undesired attention. By creating a business persona, you can control your space better than if you travel, say, looking like Madonna. Men are unlikely to suggest a wild night on the town to a woman clad in a proper conservative business suit.

Women who'd rather not spend the evening in the Convent Hilton have to develop some coping strategies and obtain a modicum of consideration from men. To begin with, men must accept a woman's sovereign right to be alone. Greta Garbo had it, and today's traveling businesswomen deserve no less. Women, for their part, must declare their independence. This begins with asserting their right *not* to eat alone in their rooms.

When a woman ventures out alone, she has the prerogative of accepting or declining male attention. Some men generously offer to join a woman eating or drinking alone because they assume she must be "lonely." A tactful explanation ("Someone will be joining me later.") or a definite, no-nonsense "No, thank you" will usually suffice. If a man or woman politely asks to share your table, accept only because you want to. Occasionally, you'll be glad you did.

Once in a very nice hotel restaurant/bar, I got into a discussion with a friendly waitress named Stephanie. I told her that I hated to sit in my hotel room but that men always hassled me when I went into restaurants alone. Having men come over to talk, try to sit with me, ask me to dance, was in some ways flattering, but mostly it was a hassle.

Later that evening a very nice man came over and said that our friendly waitress, Stephanie, had told him about a very nice woman in the corner who liked to dance and talk but did not want to be hassled. Would I care to dance—with no hassling? It turned out to be a lovely evening—with no hassling.

It *is* possible for a woman traveling alone to have positive experiences with strangers. But it's essential for her to maintain control over the situation. Split rounds or tabs, drink sparingly, and limit the evening in advance ("Don't forget the business breakfast tomorrow at 7 a.m.!") If a man won't take no as an answer from *you*, make him take it from the maitre d' or bartender.

Aside from hassles from fellow diners, women hesitate going to restaurants by themselves—both on the road and back home—because they feel they get treated like second-class citizens. They complain of getting tables next to the kitchen or in remote corners of uninhabited dining rooms. They get the bum's rush or glacial service. And they are offended by the general unwelcoming attitude of the staff who seem put out by a woman's intrusion.

Lately, however, I've noticed vast improvement in restaurants all over the country. The personnel of most good restaurants these days, particularly hotel dining rooms and restaurants frequented by businesspeople, have been instructed to take special care of single female diners. As a rule of thumb the higher the quality of the restaurant, the better it treats unaccompanied female guests.

Once you decide on a restaurant where you think it would be safe to go it alone, make a reservation—even though you may be turned down. Some restaurants don't accept reservations for "solitaires" during peak dining hours. So be it. Go early, go late, or go somewhere else. But if the restaurants accepts your reservation, you can assume the staff will act like they're glad to see you.

If you aren't completely satisfied, don't hesitate to complain. If you don't like your table, politely—but firmly—request another one. If the service isn't up to par, tell the maitre d' or, better yet, tell the owner if he or she is around. All restaurants live and die on word-of-mouth, and none can endure dissatisfied customers.

❦

As the presence of women in the executive ranks increases, so do the occasions for men and women in the same company to travel together on business. No one needs to be uncomfortable with this. The problems that may arise are usually logistical, clerical, and technical ones that can be anticipated and solved with a modicum of advanced planning.

WHO PAYS? One issue that regularly comes up is who physically pays —since it's the company that ultimately foots the bill—for restaurant meals, drinks, taxis, and other incidentals. It's really just a formality but there is a protocol to follow.

If a superior is traveling with a lower-level employee, the superior—regardless of gender—usually picks up the tab. For the sake of convenience the lower-ranking employee may occasionally pay for a minor expenditures like snacks or taxis. If the two travelers are of equal rank, decide in advance who pays for *everything*. Under no circumstances should the matter be discussed in the presence of a client nor should you ever split the check.

WHO CARRIES THE LUGGAGE? If the luggage is small and light (as it should be), the man and woman should each carry their own. If one of you has a larger case, use a folding luggage cart or a suitcase with built-in wheels, or find a porter (admittedly no mean feat). Also, luggage-wise, you need to reach a consensus on the carry-on versus check-in issue before you reach the airport.

WHO MAKES DECISIONS? The boss, naturally, regardless of gender— just like back at the office.

Also keep in mind that the junior defers to the senior in matters great and small. This ranges from grabbing the jump seat or middle seat in a limo or car to agreeing with the superior in the presence of outsiders.

It is neither necessary nor desirable to engage in long, personal conversations over the course of the trip. It is a business trip, and business is the only thing you really have to talk about.

Moreover, you are not obliged to spend any free time that might be available with your co-workers. It's perfectly all right to have dinner on your own, go out with acquaintances in the area, or just sneak away to a movie. Just let your companions know your plans in advance and, if you are the junior party, make sure you obtain your superior's permission.

The woman who is stopping at a hotel alone will find it convenient to entertain visitors in the hotel drawing rooms. Even if she has her own private sitting room, it is not good taste for her to welcome men visitors there—unless, of course, she is traveling with a chaperon.

—LILLIAN EICHLER, *NEW BOOK OF ETIQUETTE* (1934)

Meetings in your room? Between men and women? Shocking! The old etiquette books forbid them, but I find that handled properly they can be extremely useful.

Since I have traveled so much with men and—for many years with the same men—I appreciate the freedom of being able to go to each other's room for a meeting or to pick up a file or just to relax between appointments. Often, it doesn't make good business sense to meet in public areas like hotel lobbies or coffee shops.

One proviso: Early in my career, inviting a male colleague into my room for *any* reason would have been totally out of the question. And for young women just starting out in business, it is still ill-advised.

The important thing about having meetings in your room—regardless of the gender of the participants—is to create a businesslike atmosphere. Put away clothing and personal items. Clear off all desk-, dresser-, and tabletops. Open the drapes. Make sure the bed is made (but not turned down).

Then—this is slick—place a request for a wake-up call for whenever *you're* ready to call it a night with workaholic Bob. When the phone rings, your need for a little privacy—and the lateness of the hour—provide the perfect excuse to end the evening.

THE RULE OF BUSINESS TRAVEL ATTIRE FOR WOMEN AND MEN IS A VERY SIMPLE ONE: DRESS FOR TRAVEL THE WAY YOU DRESS FOR BUSINESS.

Finally, three words of advice about getting romantically involved with a colleague you're travelling with: Don't. Do. It.

No matter what you think or anybody says, somebody back at the office *will* find out and it *will* affect the way you work together. There aren't too many absolutely unbreakable rules in business life. This is one!

❧❧❧

The rule of business travel attire for women and for men is a very simple one: dress for travel the way you dress for business. I feel very strongly that when you are travelling on business, whether on your own time or on company time, you should wear appropriate business attire. You represent the company all the time and you should look the part. By looking the part, you act the part and will be accepted in most instances in that manner.

The key is not to overdress or underdress. Take a suit or two to wear on the plane and at meetings and seminars. Suits are also appropriate attire for dinner.

At least a day before you go, consider carefully what baggage you need to take, and have it packed. Take just as little as possible.
—THOS. E. HILL, *HILL'S MANUAL OF SOCIAL AND BUSINESS FORMS* (1878)

Traveling light is a matter of both good manners and good business. "Travel lean and mean," advises Lois Wyse in *Company Manners*. "Translated, that means, 'When you travel, lean on no one, and mean business.'"

For women, the lighter the suitcase, the less likely you'll need a luggage-carrying device or someone to help you carry or lift it. Limit your luggage to the carry-on variety—carry-on suitcase plus handbag or briefcase—and you will thank yourselves at critical junctures throughout the journey. You will avoid lines at the airport baggage check-in area. When the plane touches ground, you can avoid the runaround at the baggage carousel. You can grab taxis ahead of more encumbered rivals, and you can give the airport shuttle buses a run for their money.

Remember, however, that it is very bad manners—and against airline regulations—to lumber onto a plane with larger-than-carry-on-sized luggage. Your gear must be small enough to squeeze into the overhead luggage compartment or under the seat in front of you.

Frequent business travelers usually keep a carry-on outfit in readiness for unexpected departures. A typical travel readiness kit should include enough fresh underwear and socks/stockings for two days on the road, a toiletries kit, sleepwear, and a business suit that can also be worn during the evening if necessary. Shirts, ties, and other accessories can be tossed in at the last minute.

Harsh though they may be, the rigors of today's business travel offer absolutely no excuse for abandoning civil behavior. Everyone merits courteous treatment. Airline agents are hardly responsible for the blizzard in Denver that cancelled your flight (much less the unconsummated deal that ruined the trip to Phoenix). Flight agents or attendants are not your servants. Berating them in front of other travelers may vent your frustration, but it won't get you home in time for dinner. Rude behavior to airline personnel, like inappropriate dress, only reflects poorly on you and the company you represent.

Considerate behavior is just as important once you're on board the plane. An airline seat is not an office, and a commercial jet is not a private jet. I'm always surprised at how many traveling businesspeople—men and women—seem unaware of this.

On a flight recently a man sitting across the aisle from me carefully stowed his overcoat in the overhead luggage compartment, pulled out his tray table, and arranged his notebook computer in an orderly manner. A cellular phone materialized but, just as he started punching in numbers, the flight attendant came over and said he couldn't use the phone because it interfered with radio frequencies. He huffed that *other* airlines let him use the phone on the ground, demanded the flight attendant's name, and vowed to report her to (his old friend) the president of the airline.

Immediately following take-off, he lurched forward and seized the in-flight phone—which he proceeded to use unceasingly for the entire cross-country trip. Everyone within four rows in all directions was treated to a 2,500-mile cacophony of shouting, whining, instructions, and threats. I had never heard of the man's company before. But I am certain that neither I nor anybody compelled to listen to the intimate details of its affairs will ever forget its name—or the boorish performance by one of its executives.

ℭℰℑℛℯ

I'll conclude this chapter with a brief look at one peculiar subspecies of business travel: the convention. The ambience of conventions has changed markedly in recent years, due in no small part to the increased number of women in attendance. The image of "conventioneers" (the term itself has gone out of fashion) as whoopee-cushion-wielding wild men out on a spree is as out of date as the one of the boss chasing his secretary around his desk.

Today's conventions are for the most part serious conferences and trade shows, with a bit of entertainment on the side. Still, there are rules of decorum of which "attendees" (the acceptable term) should be aware.

Conventional Wisdom

* *Attend the sessions.* Take notes, ask questions—make sure your company gets the bang for the buck it spends to send you there. If you're an exhibitor at the trade show, make sure someone is always stationed in your booth.

* *Make contacts.* Introduce yourself to all you encounter. Have plenty of business cards on hand, and distribute them freely. Make notations on the back of the cards describing the contact and substance of your conversation, and follow up on them.

* *Do talk to strangers.* Regard formal sessions and any group meals as opportunities for making new acquaintances. Nothing is easier or more natural than striking up a conversation with the person sitting next to you.

* *Watch your drinking.* Even in quasi-social situations, don't forget you're "on duty." Hospitality suites can get downright inhospitable if you overstay your welcome.

* *Express appreciation.* If you are particularly impressed by a speaker or a session, make it your business to thank the parties responsible. If you don't have a chance to speak to them at the meeting, write them a note of appreciation afterwards. If you enjoy the entire meeting, write the meeting planner a thank-you note.

❖ *It's not* all *business.* The only really good reason for attending conventions is to make personal contacts, much of which occurs outside conference rooms and off exhibit floors. Partake of group dinners or other after-hours activities with other attendees. Having a businesslike meal alone with members of the opposite sex is no sin; after all, networking is one of your main reasons for being there. It would be a terrible waste of your time and the company's money if you spent the night alone in your hotel room with no networking before retiring to your room.

HIRE EDUCATION

Job Interviews as Courtesy Calls

Whether you are looking for a job or are in the position of hiring someone new, you should be especially conscious of your manners throughout the employment interview.

　　　　　　　—JACQUELINE DUNCKEL, *BUSINESS ETIQUETTE TODAY* (1987)

When I interview a job applicant, I am first interested in how he presents himself. How does he look; how is he dressed; what does he say; how does he answer my questions?

　　　　　　　—FRANKLIN MURPHY, CHAIRMAN, TIMES-MIRROR (1973)

This chapter begins with a disclaimer: I am not a human resources specialist. I can't tell you how to write a dynamite resume. I don't know how you would go about finding the best company in America you could possibly work for. I have no advice to impart on getting that all-important foot in the front door.

I will assume you already have a heart-stopping resume, have composed a cover letter Shakespeare would envy, and bear a reputation for all-around awesomeness within the industry. Consequently, the company of your dreams has invited you for an interview and you need to brush up on your manners enough to get through it alive.

Good manners are vital for job interviews. Indeed, interviewers mind *your* manners very closely and may view them as more important determinants than education, experience, or references of whether you can handle the job. Resumes don't describe your manners. Employers have to observe you up close and personal to determine how you are to work with and how well you'd blend into the corporate culture. In fact, concern about an applicant's manners is one of the main reasons they still use job interviews instead of computers to hire people.

Make no mistake: There is no occasion (except possibly a first date) on which your manners will be more closely scrutinized. People—and not just the person or persons who interview you, but everybody you encounter—are paying close attention not only to what you do and say, but how you do it, how you say it, what you're wearing, and the overall impression you create.

Yes, it is a stressful situation, but good manners—really just paying extra-close attention to the same manners that apply in other business situations—are guaranteed to see you through.

⤜⟡⤏

GOOD JOB INTERVIEWS BEGIN WITH THOROUGH PREPARATION. It's good manners and good sense to learn all you can about the company you hope to work for. This will impress the interviewer, and it's only fair that you know as much about the company you may work for as it knows about you.

Find out in advance what the company does and something about its philosophy for doing it; the age of the company and how it got started; the size of the company in terms of revenue and employees; location of major units; identity of subsidiaries, parent companies, and other affiliated concerns. Check out hiring practices and policies.

Where do you get this information? Publicly held companies publish annual reports that include most of it. Or you can find it in *Dun & Bradstreet, Standard & Poor's,* and the *Standard Directory of Advertisers,* available in most good libraries. While you're there, check out the *Reader's Guide to Periodical Literature* to determine whether *Fortune, Forbes, Business Week,* or kindred publications have written anything about your prospective employer lately. Also consult the indexes to the *Wall Street Journal* and *New York Times* for citations.

If possible, determine in advance the identity of the person who will interview you. Ask the secretary how to pronounce his or her last name and, if it's a her, whether she prefers Ms., Miss, or Mrs. This is important because unless specifically instructed to do otherwise, Ms. or Mr. is the way you will address them.

Once you know all you can find out about the company—and have a strong positive idea of the training and skills that make you supremely qualified for the position—fill your briefcase with all the necessary paperwork. Carry several copies of your resume. The one you already sent might have been misplaced, plus the personnel department and other people who interview you might want copies of their own.

Bring copies of any articles written by you or about you, references to you in company publications, letters written in your praise. If your work involves a product that fits into a briefcase, bring a sample. Don't leave home without something to write on and something to write with in case you need to make notes.

Prepare a list of references, up to six former supervisors, teachers, co-workers, business associates—but no relatives, neighbors, or social friends—who can be trusted to put in a good word. Tip them off that they might get a call. Also be prepared to encounter applications that demand dates and addresses ranging back to high school, antediluvian jobs, and other forgotten minutia.

⚜

DRESSING RIGHT FOR A JOB INTERVIEW. This is very simple—if you're a man. The uniform consists of dark suit, usually charcoal or dark blue; conservative tie; black shoes; black socks.

The only thing simple for women is determining what *not* to wear. The list includes spike heels and sandals, fishnet stockings, short skirts, pants, low-cut blouses, anything sexy. Most business fashion experts recommend "stylish but conservative," which translates into a stylish business suit in a conservative color, scant but tasteful jewelry and accessories, low-heeled pumps. The conservative dictum also applies to make-up. Keep it subtle. You don't run across many Tammy Faye lookalikes in corporate office settings.

Neatness counts when you're dressing for the part. Shoes should be freshly shined, nails cleaned and manicured, men's cheeks newly shaven, hair in place.

The rules for a job interview are the same for an experienced manager as they are for a college graduate.

—LETITIA BALDRIDGE

RULE NUMBER ONE: DON'T BE LATE. In fact, it's not a bad idea to arrive up to ten minutes early. Many jobs have been lost because applicants failed to arrive on time. Interviewees who show up late have in effect failed their first assignment. No excuse is good enough. Obviously, you should try not to postpone an interview. If you have to, however, do so as far ahead of time as possible.

ACTIVATE INTERVIEW MANNERS THE MOMENT YOU WALK INTO THE BUILD-ING. Treat everyone you encounter, from the building security guard to the company receptionist, with respect and consideration. Good companies respect the opinions of all their people. You never know who might be asked to weigh in with an impression of you. Be especially attentive to receptionists who may be strategically situated to perform (or fail to perform) critical services on your behalf.

SHAKE HANDS WITH EVERYONE TO WHOM YOU ARE INTRODUCED. When you meet your interviewer, offer your hand and include his or her name in your greeting: "I'm pleased to meet you, Mrs. Campbell."

BE ENTHUSIASTIC AND POSITIVE about the job and about the company. Use your exhaustive research to cite its recent achievements, high industry ratings, exemplary dividends, awards. Keep in mind that this isn't *really* a first date so it's the wrong time to play hard-to-get. Don't act laid-back, distracted, bored. Even if *it sounds* like the interviewer might be trying to sell the job to you, you both know that that is hardly the case.

Job Interviews: A Dozen Don'ts

1. **Don't speak badly of past or present employers.** More than just bad manners, it's bad strategy. Bitterness, complaining, willingness to assign blame are seldom listed as qualifications for a job. Moreover, since we know it's a very small world—and you surely work in a very small industry—your interviewer may well be acquainted with your ex or present boss. They could be good buddies.

   One of the toughest hurdles of any job interview is explaining why you left your last job (or wish to leave your present one) in a way that does not reflect badly on your previous employer or yourself. This feat will require a bit of advance thought and impromptu diplomacy—but those are valuable skills for any job you seek.

2. **Don't speak badly of interviewers or their companies.** I hope I don't need to explain why you shouldn't make fun of your interviewer's tie or laugh at her dress. However, the no-negativity rule extends to everything that touches upon the company and the interview experience: the company's offices, the building that houses them (including the ugly lobby and slow-moving elevator), the surrounding neighborhood, the parking situation, the trouble you had finding the place, the traffic on the way. As mother always said, if you can't say anything nice, don't say anything at all.

   The reason for the negativity embargo here is basically the same as for the last point: You don't want to sound like a whiner, a complainer, a negative person. If you have to say something negative about something, complain about the weather. If the weather is flawless, point out that it can't last.

3. **Don't sit.** Don't get off your feet until the interviewer invites you to do so and indicates where. If no seat is indicated, choose one opposite the interviewer. While sitting, don't slouch.

4. **Don't smoke.** Don't light up without an invitation. Even if there's an ashtray on hand, you better wait until the interviewer invites you to use it. If you do smoke and don't want to announce the fact prematurely, make sure the odor on your clothes doesn't give away your secret. You may not notice any smell, but a non-smoker's nose will. If you are asked whether you smoke, tell the truth but express willingness to comply with the strictures of today's smoke-free workplace.

5. **Don't wear cologne/perfume/after-shave.** Overscented applicants rank near the top of job interviewer complaint lists. It sounds like a pet peeve, but it could torpedo your hopes. It's almost impossible for a person to determine how much scent is too much. Don't take chances; do without.

6. **Don't put anything on the interviewer's desk.** This breach of courtesy violates their personal space. Similarly, don't take anything from the interviewer's desk, and don't read (or at least don't get caught reading) anything on the desk.

7. **Don't hesitate to blow your own horn.** This is essentially a sales call; the product is yourself. Successful salespeople draw attention to a product's virtues and downplay its deficiencies. If you're not

THERE IS NO OCCASION ON WHICH YOUR MANNERS WILL BE MORE CLOSELY
SCRUTINIZED. PEOPLE ARE PAYING CLOSE ATTENTION NOT ONLY TO WHAT
YOU DO AND SAY, BUT HOW YOU DO IT, HOW YOU SAY IT, WHAT YOU'RE WEARING,
AND THE OVERALL IMPRESSION YOU CREATE.

comfortable with outright bragging, couch self-praise in the third person (as plural as possible): "Supervisors say I'm reliable, efficient, trustworthy, good to my mother . . ." "My clients tell me I'm the only person in the company they'll do business with."

Similarly, don't be overmodest in regard to any of your accomplishments the interviewer may cite. If the interviewer mentions an extraordinarily youthful ascent to a position of great authority, don't say, "My dad is president of the company." Instead say, "It was a real challenge and a terrific learning experience."

8. **Don't ramble.** Answer questions fully but succinctly. Don't add extraneous material to answers to questions on which they have no bearing. That's rude, and it may make it sound like you didn't understand the question.

9. **Don't reveal that you don't know what you want to do with your life.** Job interviewers are not career counselors. Their role is to fill a need within their company, not find ways to help the company fulfill you. For the sake of the interview, assume you know where you want to go and that this particular job with this particular company is absolutely the best way to get there.

10. **Don't sound disappointed if the job falls short of expectations.** Burn no bridges. Feign enthusiasm even if the job is less than you'd hoped for. Consider whether the real job might turn out to have advantages over the imagined one. You also might be able to negotiate some improvements in the job description.

11. **Don't lie.** You might exaggerate your policy-making authority or embellish your role in designing your company's most successful product. You can inflate the number of people under your direct supervision and maybe even gussy up a title. Those lies are misdemeanors, mere parking tickets, part of the game. But lies about degrees, certifications, awards, the very existence of certain jobs are something else: capital crimes punishable by the job-seeker's equivalent of death. Don't lie about anything that can be easily checked out. If you were fired, admit it, explain it, but omit the gory details. Account for gaps in employment, but don't cook the dates or manufacture nonexistent jobs.

12. **Don't ask about salary.** Most job-search experts advise applicants not to mention salary until you receive a firm job offer. If the interviewer asks about your salary requirements, offer a range but not a vast one. Those who claim they can live on salaries of between $20,000 and $80,000 a year may not be viewed as serious candidates. Indicate extenuating circumstances that might make the lower amount acceptable—prospects for promotion, bonuses, travel, no travel. But make sure your minimum amount is something you can live with—because chances are good that's how much you'll be offered.

Questions to Answer

Outside of specifics related to you, your past or present job, and your experience in the industry, job applicants must be prepared to answer certain standard extra-resume questions straight out of the hirer's handbook:

❖ **What are your strengths regarding the position you are applying for?** This is an opportunity for strategic bragging. Don't waste it by reading back your resume. Link your experience to the specific requirements of the job at hand.

❖ **What are your weaknesses?** Since you must say *something*, come up with weaknesses that highlight your strengths: I work too hard, care too much, take my work too seriously, sometimes suspect I may be turning into a . . . *workaholic!*

❖ **What kind of people do you have trouble working with?** The kind of people you have trouble working with are, of course, the kind of people the company doesn't want around anyway, i.e., lazy people, careless people, clock-watchers, people who don't give a hoot about their work, disloyal people, etc.

❖ **What job situations or conditions make you uneasy?** Don't go astray here and blurt out something about pressure situations, when you don't get credit for what you do, demanding employers. Prepare a relatively benign response—"I get uneasy when my work isn't challenging/creative/demanding enough"—but don't lay it on too thick.

❖ **Tell me about yourself.** This isn't a question: it's an invitation to self-destruct. It's a form of free association, which was invented by Freud—and you know what *he* found out about people. Obviously, this calls for an individualized response. I can only warn you to have your story straight before you begin to speak.

Questions Not to Answer?

Notice the question mark at the end of this subtitle. This isn't "upspeak" (see Chapter 4); it's there because, given the unequal nature of the interviewer-interviewee relationship, I'm not sure you can afford not to answer *any* question.

The Equal Opportunity Employment Act and the American With Disabilities Act prohibit discrimination based on age, race, religion, national origin, marital status, and disabilities or medical history. But this doesn't mean you won't be asked about such matters, or that the wrong answer won't disqualify you for the job.

Interviewers might also inquire about credit status, arrest or conviction record, sexual preference, and workers' compensation claims. Women with children are likely to be asked about their child-care responsibilities. Women without children may be asked to assess the likelihood of having them, even what if any birth-control methods they use.

Do you have to respond to this kind of question? Probably yes. Even the most mannerly refusals will make interviewers assume the worst. And it would be extremely difficult to prove in court that your refusal to answer one particular question was the reason you weren't hired.

My advice is to answer these questions as honestly as you can—and then ask yourself a much more significant one: Is a company that asks these kind of questions the kind of company I want to work for?

"Do You Have Any Questions?"

Near the conclusion of the interview, the interviewer will turn the tables and invite you to ask about the company or the job. Ask intelligent insightful questions that indicate your interest in a *long-term* relationship with the company. Specific questions may come to mind about the identity and nature of your prospective supervisor and department. You may be curious about the identity of potential co-workers. Other generic questions include:

❖ What are the opportunities for promotion?

❖ Are any training programs available?

❖ What would be a typical career track for someone starting in this position?

Feel free to inquire about the mechanics of the job search:

❖ How long have you been interviewing for this position?

❖ How many candidates will you interview?

❖ When will you make a decision?

❖ What can I do to improve my chances of getting this job?

Don't Ask . . .

Just as insightful intelligent questions enhance your appeal, the wrong questions can be real turn-offs:

❖ **Don't ask about benefits.** Just as you shouldn't broach the subject of salary until you've received a firm job offer, it is equally inappropriate to inquire about insurance benefits, vacation time, bonuses, raise schedules, and other perks. These are *fringe* benefits, not the basis for making a decision.

❖ **Don't ask about sick time or family leave.** You don't want to sound like someone who expects to need a lot of time off.

❖ **Don't ask about the social scene.** This includes the number of single women/men who work there, whether there's a company softball team, company picnics, and other extracurricular activities.

❖ **Don't ask embarrassing questions.** Your interviewer will not be in a position to respond to EPA chemical waste dumping charges or explain why the company stock dropped 35 points during the last quarter.

❖ **Don't ask if the company contemplates building a new plant in Mexico.**

After-Interview Etiquette

THANK-YOU NOTES

Within two days of the interview, be sure to send the interviewer a thank-you note. It's an essential element of business etiquette and a document for your personnel file. The thank-you note assures the interviewer that you're still interested in the job. If you're not interested, send one anyway. A better job may come up later, and you never know where your path and the interviewer's might cross again.

Although it's called a "note," use standard-sized high-quality business stationery and the formal business-letter format. Keep it short—two or three paragraphs will do and definitely no more than one page.

First, thank the interviewer for spending the time with you. Reemphasize your interest in the job, how much you enjoyed learning about the company, how much you want to work there.

Recall a particular topic of conversation that came up during the interview. Perhaps you discovered a personal connection: you attended the same college, used to work at the same place, enjoy the same leisure pursuits, have acquaintances in common. If this connection produced something you laughed about, so much the better.

Finally, re-assert your qualification for the job. No hard sell, just a reminder that you have the background they're looking for and the enthusiasm to succeed.

CALLING BACK

The hiring process moves very slowly, especially if you're anxious to find out if you've got the job. Don't panic even if you've heard nothing weeks after what you thought was a sensational interview. No news is no news.

During the interview, remember, you did ask when a decision would be made. When that period expires, it's quite acceptable to phone the interviewer to ask what's happened. If nothing has happened, you have yet another opportunity to express your interest.

If you're told that the decision will be made by a certain time, call back then. But watch your manners, and make sure you always stay on the right side of the fine line that separates avid job-seeker from obnoxious pest.

PROFESSIONAL COURTESY

*Drawing the Line Between Your Work
and Your Life*

*In social life—and in business life too, though less pronouncedly—
we seek the people with whom we can be at ease, the people whose
manners do not offend us, and in whose company we feel entirely
comfortable.*

—LILLIAN EICHLER, *THE NEW BOOK OF ETIQUETTE* (1924)

*The grind of day-to-day office life requires the same empathy and tact
that is required to live year in and year out with one's family . . . The
same good manners that carry you through the vagaries of domestic
life will serve you well in the office.*

—MARJABELLE YOUNG STEWART, *THE NEW ETIQUETTE* (1987)

 ow often have you heard this? "We're all *family* here at Itsthepitz
Corporation." Ah, yes. As one of Hemingway's characters dryly re-
marked, "Isn't it pretty to think so."

The office environment of the '90s has become a very informal place.
Bosses and subordinates freely address each other by their first names. Intimate personal secrets form the substance of water-cooler banter. Football
pools occupy as much of the work day as work. And each routine event—
birthdays, anniversaries, important holidays like Friday—become an excuse for an office-wide celebration.

Amiable people that we are, Americans have trouble separating our
professional lives from our social lives. This leads to conflicting assump-
tions. Being friendly with someone in the context of the office does not
make you part of their inner circle. The mild flirting that seems as essential to office survival as coffee breaks should not be mistaken as an expression of serious romantic interest (though sometimes it may be).

What goes at home, among family and social friends or at parties, definitely does not go at the office. The line-crossing confusion between social
manners and business manners manifests itself in many many ways.

A kiss is just a kiss.

—HERMAN HUPFELD, "AS TIME GOES BY"

I'd like to add an dissonant lyric: A kiss *is* just a kiss—unless the kiss takes place in a business situation. Then a kiss may be a serious breach of professionalism. A woman who gratefully accepts a "social kiss" at a party or upon meeting outside friends of either sex may recoil at any attempts at kissing in a business situation and feel patronized by them.

The question as to whether it is ever proper for colleagues to kiss in a business situation is not an easy one to answer. The answer is . . . maybe.

Workplace hugs can be forgiven when they spontaneously erupt to celebrate once-in-a-lifetime events: landing that big account, a promotion, or winning the lottery.

Less easier to handle than business kissers are co-workers who seek to share their intimate confidences with you. A person with whom, socially, you might be happy to commiserate at length, strains your patience in the office. There's a line to be observed and, invisibly, he or she has crossed it.

While most people can understand why kisses may be verboten, fending off interpersonal confidences is greeted with less good will. If you care about them as people, how can you possibly refuse to listen to their secrets? Apparently, you do not care about them. They won't like that, and the animosity could strain your working relationship.

Unfortunately, once colleagues have cried on your shoulder it's too late to give them a cold one. The best strategy is to anticipate unwanted confidences, deter, delay, demur, scramble—but avoid direct confrontations.

Often, a colleague will ask permission to escalate the relationship to higher levels of intimacy. "Can I talk to you about something personal?" What do you say? Just saying "no" sounds much too cold. But if you say "Shoot," "I'm all ears," or "It's your nickel," you'll never hear the end of it.

Instead devise ingenious ways to not say no but also not to listen. "Not right now, I have to make an important phone call," or "I'm sorry, this isn't really a good time for me." Do this a few times and they should get the message.

AMIABLE PEOPLE THAT WE ARE, AMERICANS HAVE TROUBLE SEPARATING OUR PROFESSIONAL LIVES FROM OUR SOCIAL LIVES.

The most important factor, office-relationship-wise, is to stay out of situations where you tell people you won't to listen to their problems *anymore*. That puts you in the position of a cruel, uncaring, insensitive, utterly rotten person *who knows their most intimate secrets*. This combustible combination of elements can produce conflagrations of retribution and intra-office misery. The exchange rate for an ounce of prevention here is much higher than the usual pound of cure.

The fine line of professionalism that theoretically separates business life and social life is really the same line that distinguishes "friendship" from "friendly." It is acceptable and highly desirable to be *friendly* with the people you work with. Greet them by name each day the first time you see them, nod when you encounter them later on, know the basic facts of their *curriculum vitae* (i.e., if they're single or married, have children, where they live), celebrate or mourn their passages, do lunch, do drinks, maybe get together occasionally after work with your partners. But reserve true *friendship* for people you know exclusively outside the office.

The workplace is hardly fertile breeding ground for friendship. The best friendships are founded on common interests, a similar way of looking at the world, and above all else equality. In a work environment, how many relationships are truly equal? Isn't one person always a little higher on the company totem pole? Won't one have a smidgeon more seniority or seem to be moving a tad more swiftly to the top?

Even if co-workers are equal, they are likely to be in competition. And if two friends are equal *now*, promotion, demotion, restructuring, or a disastrous third quarter can end equality fast. If your office friend's career turns into a disaster, you won't want to be poisoned with incompetence by association.

I don't want any yes-men around me. I want everybody to tell me the truth even if it costs them their jobs.

—SAMUEL GOLDWYN

The trickiest area of inter-office friendship involves relationships between employee and boss. Employees who bend over backwards to cultivate friendships with superiors will undoubtedly curry the disfavor of peers. Bosses should be leery too. How can they tell the difference between true friendship and good old-fashioned brown-nosing?

Neither are bosses' motives above suspicion or reproach. Friendships between employees and their supervisors may be hazardous to the employee's professional health because often supervisors cultivate personal relationships with promising underlings for less-than-noble reasons.

Managers may use favored employees as "moles" who tell them what's really going on in their departments. Friendly employees can be also be powerful office political allies. If the superior and employee are of the opposite sex, there is always a risk that the boss will assert his or her authority to obtain sexual favors, a turn of events that can lead to charges of sexual harassment (see Chapter 9).

Despite inherent dangers—mainly for the employee that the end of the friendship may lead to the end of the unemployment line—supervisor-employee friendship may not be an entirely bad thing. A close relationship with a supervisor can be a worthwhile experience that permits employees to develop top-level contacts, gives them an inside look at how management decisions are made, and grooms them for a leadership role. The employer and the boss may even wind up with a friend for the rest of their lives.

⋯⋰✳⋱⋯

Romances between co-workers are one of the most troublesome of today's working relationships. Once strictly taboo, office romances have become an awkward fact of business life. The real problem about office romances is that they affect not only the persons involved in the affair but everybody who works with them, over them, and under them.

Since office romances cannot be banned, a code of etiquette must be formulated for dealing with them. First, if you are having an affair you must determine the discretion-index of your particular work environment. In some offices, couples are well-advised to engage in maximum security. They can make absolutely sure no "people will say we're in love" by telling *absolutely no one* about the existence of the affair. They can arrange encounters in remote hideaways unlikely to be frequented by the gang from the office, and they can arrive at work separately after they've spent the night together. This level of caution is also advisable anywhere when either or both the lovers are married or the relationship involves people with great disparities in company stature.

Unfortunately, secret affairs seldom remain secret for very long. Someone will notice something—a blush, a touch, a glance that lasts a millisecond too long—and demand confirmation or denial. Secret love affairs by definition involve two people in a highly charged emotional state. Such people are more than likely to express their emotions with unexpected, unexplainable, and unprofessional lapses from habitual behavior. In other words, they will do strange things that call attention to themselves and it won't be long before people will say they're in love.

Thrilling though they may be, secret affairs may be hazardous or fatal to your career. I can't command you to refrain under all circumstances, but I will advise you to stay away from them if you possibly can.

The lion's share of office romances, however, take place between un-married people of more or less equal rank who, except for working at the same place, have no reason *not* to be involved with each other. The code of behavior for them is to walk a line that avoids subterfuge and the least im-plication of sneakiness yet does not rub their romance in their co-workers' faces. This couple may arrive at work together, but they should never be spotted hugging, kissing, or gazing upon one another with longing. They can refer to their outside activities but never, together or separately, de-scribe the details of their sex life to anyone in the office.

Most important, they should not do anything that gives colleagues reason to suspect the romance has any impact on their job performance. This means not spending hours of the workday engaged in non-produc-tive private conversation, not being too quick to praise your sweetheart, or not seeming too eager to promote your loved one's concepts. Don't let your lover's rival become your rival. Don't let jealousy cloud professional judgment.

Admittedly, these are very difficult things for human beings to do—and explain why office romances used to be seriously taboo. Frequently, workplace love affairs force one of the lovers into a position so compromis-ing that he or she must choose between the job and the relationship. It's a decision that has to be made coolly, carefully, and correctly; if it isn't handled well, you can lose both your lover and your job.

How should supervisors deal with a company romance? If the romance has no detrimental effect on the individuals' job performance and doesn't lower workplace morale, supervisors aren't obliged to do anything. If it does affect their work, action must be taken.

Tactfulness is essential. Summon the employee into your office for a warning. Explain the performance-related cause for your dissatisfaction. Justify your displeasure with facts and figures. Do *not* attribute their lower performance to the affair, and in no way indicate disapproval of their love life. Limiting your explicit complaint to work behavior may—if you ever have to dismiss them—save you from a lawsuit.

Managers, even more than other co-workers, should avoid getting pulled into affairs between underlings. Don't counsel either party, don't encourage or discourage the relationship. If either of them is married, don't cover for your employee—by saying they're in a meeting, on a sales call, in the rest room, etc.—but don't let the spouse pry information out of you.

꧁✢꧂

Office parties, one of the great oxymorons of working life, are great erasers of the line between professional and private lives. Office parties are also great generators of the aforementioned interoffice romances, not to mention couplings of much more temporary duration.

Christmas season is the great time for office parties, the time when most businesses feel obliged to host some sort of celebration for the staff. But parties can take place throughout the year: on other national or local holidays, to commemorate company anniversaries, or celebrate extraordinary company achievements. Office parties can be held on company premises, in restaurants, or in hotels. They can occur during office hours, during lunch, after hours, or over the weekend. A picnic is one species of office party; so are management-sponsored excursions.

Whenever, wherever, whyever they occur, office parties are dangerous because they deliberately blur the line between business and social life. Which rules are in effect? Business manners or social manners?

You are in a party setting, eating, drinking, perhaps telling jokes and dancing. Yet these are the people you've worked with all week—and will have to work with again next Monday morning. Under these disorienting circumstances, getting through the party unscathed may be tantamount to professional survival.

Seven Ways To Avoid Office Party Hangovers

1. **Arrive late, but not too late.** Come early and you seem too anxious to get away from work (or to belt down a drink). Show up over a half-hour late, however, you may be judged unpunctual for a quasi-official event.

2. **Watch your drinking.** Count your drinks and stay well below normal social party limits. Keep your glass filled—you don't want the boss to think you're unsociable—but drain it slowly.

3. **Don't tell jokes.** The life of this party may be, career-wise, dead in the water. It's almost impossible today to tell a joke that is both funny and inoffensive—Leno can't do it and Letterman doesn't try. Don't let the deceptively relaxed party atmosphere and alcohol knock the sense out of your sense of humor.

4. **Don't make a pass.** Two co-workers spend the year smoldering in silence. Finally, they "get it on" after the office Christmas party. What a cliche! Well, it wouldn't *be* a cliche if it didn't happen all the time. No good can come of this. Leave the party by yourself.

5. **Look like you're having a good time.** That means smiling, mingling, not sulking in a corner, not bending a colleague's ear about how your wife, kids, dog, investment counselor, personal trainer, etc., don't understand you. Keep the mood merry and bright.

6. **Don't talk business.** This may be tough, and it may necessitate feigning interest in sports or politics or movies or local real estate prices or other topics you know nothing and care less about. But party time is the wrong time to commit yourself even unofficially off-the-record to a position that may come back to haunt you.

7. **Leave early, but not too early.** Don't be the first to leave: It seems rude unless you have an airtight excuse. And don't be the last to go: It makes them wonder if you have a life. Rule of thumb: Take off after about one-third of the guests have already departed.

I Gave (and Gave and Gave and Gave) at the Office

One of the more dysfunctional evocations of the One Big Happy Fallacy is the proliferation of collections. Yesterday, your office mate's daughter was selling Girl Scout cookies, today they want a few bucks to buy a shower gift for the secretary in accounting, tomorrow it'll be for the boss' son's high school computer team's annual Hackathon.

Partly it's a sign of the times. Many donation requests come from parents whose kids' schools need money to fund extra-curricular and, in some cases, curricular activities. Prices are rising, too. While you used to be able to get away with buying a $5 raffle ticket, now the tariff is a $20 crate of Florida oranges or a $30 magazine subscription.

You may not like making these contributions but you may not be in a position to turn them down—not if you want to maintain a good working relationship with the person requesting the contribution or making the pitch. If they're doing it for their kids, they'll take a turndown even harder than if it involves a project of their own. The only thing worse than being pressured into compromising their professional relationships by hitting on their colleagues for a contribution is having their colleagues turn them down. They won't soon forget it.

I remember when you could only buy Girl Scout cookies from real-live Scouts who appeared on your doorstep in full dress uniform. Today, most of the cookies seem to be sold by parents of Girl Scouts to co-workers who never lay eyes on the Scout herself. I miss that. On the other hand, the quality of the cookies has markedly improved in recent years, so maybe there's something to be said for progress.

My advice is to view requests for contributions, raffle tickets, cookies, fruit, magazines, or gifts as a kind of payroll tax. The only way to avoid the assessments is for your company to institute a no-solicitation policy. If they don't, you have to decide how much you can afford to spend or if you can afford to say no.

If you lend money, you make a secret enemy; if you refuse it, an open one.
—VOLTAIRE

Borrowing and lending money is widely practiced between co-workers. Sometimes people can't make it to a cash machine or a store that cashes checks; sometimes it wouldn't matter if they could. Even if the amount is trivial—normally just enough for lunch, transportation, parking, etc.—the potential for friction is great.

If you have to borrow, do it as infrequently as possible and for as small an amount as possible. Make a note of the debt on your desk calendar or daily planner. And repay it at once: the next day or the moment you return from the cash machine is not too soon.

Proper behavior by the lender is more problematic. Is it mannerly to ask a colleague to repay a loan? If so, when is the right time to do it?

Yes, it is proper to ask for repayment, and it's the right thing to do. They may have forgotten. That's rude, but it happens all the time. I would let two days pass before asking. Any shorter might seem like you're dunning them, much longer and they might really forget.

Ask politely but firmly, "Do you have the money I lent you for lunch Tuesday?" If they don't, ask when they'll get it. If they don't pay then, ask them again. If they keep putting you off, at some point you'll have to act like a bank: close their account and never again lend them a dime.

The fine line between *all* social/business relationships is called professionalism.

DEALS OVER MEALS

The Fine Art of Business Wining and Dining

It is the most appropriate time, while you wait to be served, for you to put into practice your knowledge of small talk and pleasant words. . . . By interchange of thought, much valuable information may be acquired at the table.
—THOS. E. HILL, *HILL'S MANUAL OF SOCIAL AND BUSINESS FORMS* (1878)

More business is conducted at the dining table than ever before with the prospect of the dinner table striking terror in the hearts of otherwise polished professionals.
—MARY MITCHELL, PRESIDENT, UNCOMMON COURTESIES (1993)

ining out for business need not be a cause for alarm. While the quasi-social away-from-the-office setting does present its share of pitfalls and land mines, no aspect of business life possesses more clearly defined, coherent, and easily mastered codes of correct behavior.

Good business dining manners merely apply and amplify the good table manners all of us (I hope) were taught as children. Indeed, our parents were thinking of occasions like business meals when they were patiently teaching us our table manners. But here the stakes are a little higher. Slip up and instead of getting a dirty look or being sent to your room, you might lose a client, blow a deal, or fumble your way out of a job.

The occasions for business meals correspond with the occasions for regular meals, i.e., breakfast, lunch, and dinner, each with its own particular strategic nuance.

BREAKFAST

The business breakfast (a.k.a. power breakfast) was conceived by the New York financial community as a way to cram a little bit more business into the top of a very busy work day. Breakfast-time is also a good time to nab out-of-town visitors about to embark on a day of activities. Since they *do* cut into people's free time (and sleep), business breakfasts are never social events. They should be tightly focussed on matters of some urgency or which require more or less immediate decisions. They should get right to the point, stick to business, and be brief.

LUNCH

There's a good reason why "doing lunch" is far and away the most popular business meal. It's the ideal way to combine business and sociability. *Everybody* has to eat lunch sometime during the business day, and lunch doesn't extend the work day in either direction. It's less strictly business than an office meeting but briefer and markedly less expensive than a business dinner. Lunch also provides a relaxed but structured setting for taking a closer look at potential employees.

DINNER

Business dinners are used to deepen relationships and, because there is seldom a predetermined termination time, discuss business at some length. Business dinners are still common but less so than in the past. Businesspeople are increasingly jealous of their free time and less willing to extend the business day late into the evening. Business dinners also present logistical problems that don't exist for breakfast or lunch: What time is good for everybody's work schedule and dining habits? Should you go home and change clothes? Should you invite your spouse? And of course there's the temptation to eat too much, drink too much, and talk too much that makes dinnertime less than ideal for taking care of business.

TWILIGHT ZONE

More and more out-of-office business encounters are being scheduled in the late afternoon/early evening transition period between office and home. Perennially popular cocktail lounges have lately been supplemented by the coffee bars that have sprung up in many cities.

The latest trend is the late afternoon "power tea," a less expensive, non-alcoholic, time-efficient alternative to the power meals. Since everyone does lunch or breakfast, inviting someone to tea gets their attention, and the refined atmosphere of most settings where you'll have tea—usually elegant hotels or fine restaurants—makes it a gracious and leisurely experience. Formal tea is usually served between 2:00 p.m. and 5:00 p.m. and, yes, you can order coffee.

Certain rules and procedures govern all business meals. Everything begins with the invitation. Business meals don't just happen; someone has to initiate them, and the one who does incurs a broad range of responsibilities.

Business meals, particularly lunches, can be arranged over the telephone a few days in advance or even the morning of the lunch. The first responsibility of the inviter (henceforth known as the "host") is to provide the invitee (or "guest") a solid business reason for spending the host's company's money and both of their time. The reasons must cover not only why *any* meeting is desirable, but why the business couldn't as easily be handled in an office or over the phone.

Emily Post's Etiquette offers nine good reasons for inviting business colleagues out for a meal:

- ❖ To thank someone for a service rendered
- ❖ To celebrate a newly closed deal
- ❖ To win the confidence of a client or perspective client
- ❖ To share common problems
- ❖ To get to know someone better
- ❖ To ask a favor
- ❖ To propose or discuss ideas
- ❖ To introduce other people
- ❖ To simply get away from the office and relax.

The time of the meal is negotiated between host and guest, contingent upon local custom. In some cities, lunch is eaten at noon, period. In others areas, 12:30, 1:00, or 1:30 are the norm. Dinner hours fluctuate even more, with people in the middle part of the country perhaps preferring to eat a bit earlier than those along the coasts. Plan to spend between an hour and an hour-and-a-half at lunch, two hours at the absolute most. Dinners may sometimes be much longer.

The host selects the location, ideally a restaurant within easy reach of the guest's office. Never offer open-ended invitations, "Where do you want to go?" Instead, give the guest a choice of two restaurants that you have frequented and where you are known by the staff.

The choice of restaurant is of vital importance. Unless it is an occasion of spectacular importance, lavish establishments are inappropriate. Unless speed is a prerequisite for being able to meet at all, fast-food joints won't do. The self-service demands of cafeterias, buffets, salad bars, and smorgasbords are unsuitable when you must make effective use of your limited time together. In most instances, restaurants with efficient but unrushed table service are the best choice.

If you're not familiar with the place, make a preliminary reconnaissance to determine noise level, background music level, seating arrangements, proximity of tables (and eavesdroppers), and other potential communication barriers. Restaurants with booths make good places for business meetings.

Make a reservation, even if the restaurant doesn't demand it. It will help the restaurant recognize you when you show up and remember you the next time you call. Try to arrive a few minutes before your guest, and take a seat in the bar or at your table. In case you don't arrive first, be sure to give your guest's name to the maitre d'.

In most cases, the host pays for everything: meals, drinks, drinks the guest has before the host shows up, coat check, tips, everything. Exceptions to the host-pays convention occur when an employee asks a manager out to discuss job-related issues. Unless the employee insists, the manager should pay the tab. Two managers who eat lunch together can agree in advance to go Dutch. And customers who ask salespersons to discuss business over lunch or dinner can expect the guest to put it on the expense account.

Hostly obligations extend into the ordering process. An awkward moment occurs when the waiter asks for a drink order. Nobody wants to order an alcoholic beverage first, but no one wants not to order one first. Make sure your guest understands that the drink can be alcohol but that it doesn't have to be alcohol. "What would you like to drink? Wine? Mineral water? Juice? A Coke?" A thoughtful host now interjects his or her own order—"Make mine a triple Tanqueray martini," or "Perrier with a twist"—and gives the guest something to go on. The most important rule pertaining to the situation: nobody *has* to drink alcohol if they don't really want to.

The host also establishes standards for the meal order. Since the host has presumably eaten in the restaurant before, it is fitting for the host to offer menu recommendations. These recommendations will signal the price-range of the meal. If times are flush, the host might suggest a roasted truffle appetizer followed by the filet mignon. In reduced circumstances, the host might remark that the restaurant makes great sandwiches.

❧

What do you talk about at the beginning? Nothing that can spoil your appetite for business. Avoid ethnic subjects, unless you are both of the same background. Don't get into politics, unless it affects your business. Under all circumstances, stay away from religion.

Safe subjects include something in the news; sports; the weather; new movies, plays, or TV shows; where you live and how much it costs to live there. Do this with discretion—no bragging.

Once the meal is ordered and preliminary small talk out of the way, host and guest can finally take up the business on the table.

❧

The role of the guest at business meals is much the same as the role of guest in social contexts. Good hosts should unobtrusively take care of everything. Guests will be entertained, and in return they will be charming. But they will not make the slightest effort to pick up the check. Since all concerned know the meal is a tax-deductible business expense that comes out of no pocket more personal than the host's expense account, they owe the host heartfelt but not excessive gratitude.

Still, there are certain areas where good guest manners can expedite the flow. The moment when the invitation is tendered is the occasion to announce any dietary restrictions that would influence choice of restaurant. If you're a vegetarian, mention it. If you're boycotting a restaurant for political reasons, mention that. If it could be a problem if someone from your office spotted you with the host, identify places where that is not likely to happen.

During the meal, if the host fails to make clear the policy on alcoholic beverages, don't order one. Order something, but make it juice, mineral water, a soft drink, Virgin Mary or other "mocktail."

If the host doesn't signal the price range of the meal, stick to the middle of the menu. Unless invited to do so, back off from the Lobster Thermidor, but don't embarrass the host by bottom fishing a cheeseburger deluxe. Guests shouldn't take advantage of the situation, but they are not obliged to order anything less than a full meal.

Guests should never complain about the quality of the service or the food. If your order is wrong or improperly prepared (well-done as opposed to rare), ask your server to correct the problem but don't make your host feel responsible. On the other hand, permit your host the gratification of basking in the reflected glory of anything about the restaurant that meets with your approval.

One contemporary note: The guidelines for the use of portable phones apply equally to hosts and guest. Place or accept calls only in the event of extreme emergencies. Even then, excuse yourself from the table to make or take the call. If you have to wear a beeper or pager, turn down the volume as low as it can go.

⚜

Do roles of host and guest change when either party is a woman? Of course not. Rather, of course they *should* not. In reality, however, women have to put forth a little extra effort to obtain equal treatment.

A businesswoman who intends to be the host should make that fact unambiguously clear when she tenders the invitation. "Can we have lunch next Friday?" is not quite explicit enough; "Can I take you to lunch next Friday?" is.

She should select a restaurant, make the reservation herself in her own name, and call the guest that morning to outline the arrangements. These steps should be enough to establish the woman's role as host with the guest.

At the restaurant, she should request the menus and, in the server's hearing, invite the guest to order a drink, recommend appetizers, praise an entree. Now the server definitely knows who's who.

At the end of the meal she should ask the server for the check. If the server mistakenly delivers the bill to a male guest—and it happens all the time—she should firmly tell the server, "The check is for me." She must be polite—but equally firm—if the male guest goes for his wallet. To forestall possible post-prandial Big Macho Attacks of check-grabbing, she can give the restaurant a charge-card imprint when she arrives and quickly sign the receipt on the way out.

GUESTS WILL BE ENTERTAINED, AND IN RETURN THEY WILL BE CHARMING. BUT—
UNLIKE THIS SCENE—THEY WILL NOT MAKE THE SLIGHTEST EFFORT TO PICK UP
THE CHECK.

Woman guests must take pains to emphasize that they are business-people first, ladies second. When a man is the host, the egalitarian principles of business outrank the manners of social situations wherein deference to ladies is still the norm. Since you can't have it *both* ways, you're better off with businesslike esteem than social deference. The social amenities extended to ladies are likely to diminish your authority at a business lunch.

Amenities to dispense with include his helping you off with your coat, pulling out your chair, and standing when you approach the table. Don't expect the male host to do anything he wouldn't do if you were a man. On the other hand, don't overreact or be insulted if you are extended these courtesies.

❧❀❧

Beyond the protocol of arranging the business meal, the mechanics of eating generate considerable tension. Not only are your ideas and business acumen on display in public, so are your table manners. This is the absolute worse time to wonder which fork to use or worry about a speck of tomato sauce on your yellow tie. The spotlight shines with particularly harsh intensity when the meal is part of the job interview.

Many eating disorders are resolved by ordering the right dish. Assuming that food is absolutely the least important part of the business meal, the strategy is to be conservative. Don't order what you crave; don't sample anything new; don't try to impress dining companions with gourmet savoir faire; don't order anything that can get you into trouble.

What Not To Order at a Business Meal

* **Don't order pasta.** Hard to eat with much dexterity. A mouth drooling spaghetti is not a pretty sight.

* **Don't order lobster.** Hard to eat, messy, expensive too. The no-lobster rule also covers hard-shell crabs and anything that requires special tools—nutcrackers, mallets, pincers, picks—for ingestion.

* **Avoid other foods that are difficult to eat.** This category includes the elusive pea, the multilayered artichoke, and asparagus spears (which, unsauced, you are permitted to eat with your fingers, but do *they* know that?)

* **Don't order anything that sounds expensive.** Along with lobster, escargot, caviar, pheasant, hummingbird tongues, or other delicacy items associated with conspicuous consumption—even if the prices they're charging aren't all that high.

* **Don't order it if you can't pronounce it correctly.** Those who *can* pronounce it correctly may be hard-pressed to stifle a snicker. Trying to dodge this bullet by pointing to the item on the menu only makes matters worse.

* **Don't use chopsticks.** Unless you wield them with perfection. Then *absolutely* don't use them lest non-chopstick-literate companions think you're showing off.

* **Don't order finger food.** Ribs, corn-on-the-cob, french fries, fried chicken, messy sandwiches, etc. Few of us look businesslike while cramming these dainties into our mouths.

- ❖ **Avoid foods with lots of garlic and raw onions.** Is an explanation necessary?

- ❖ **Don't order fish with bones.** Go with the fillet: it's hard to keep your mind on business when performing a dissection. Bony chicken can be just as tricky.

What's safe to order? Grilled meat or fish, salads, omelets, anything consisting of firm chunks easily pierced with a fork.

I will not deliver an exhaustive dissertation on proper table manners. Entire books have been written on the subject (and I know a lot of businesspeople who ought to read them). I will, however, go over some common lapses in dining etiquette on display virtually anywhere congenial businesspeople gather, of which perpetrators may be blissfully ignorant.

Bad table manners, I must note, have never been scientifically correlated with low intelligence, duplicity, laziness, unreliability, or any other negative character traits. However, fairly or unfairly, consciously or unconsciously, that won't stop people from thinking there are connections. Mealtime gaffes cannot pass unnoticed by those who know how to do it right.

A Dirty Dozen Bad Table Manners

1. **Don't "cello grasp" your fork.** Don't cradle the fork in your left hand like the aforesaid instrument. Hold it tines down, thumb under handle, with the tip of your forefinger pushing the center point at the base of the times.

2. **Don't "dagger grip" your knife.** Don't stab that steak! Hold the knife blade down, handle between middle finger and thumb about two inches above point where handle meets blade. The forefinger pressing down on the top of the blade provides the cutting force.

3. **Don't rest cutlery on the table or edge of your plate.** Once you pick up any piece of silverware, no part should come in contact with the table again.

4. **Don't butter the entire roll or cut it with knife.** Break off a chunk, butter, eat, repeat. Never lift the entire roll or slice to mouth.

5. **Don't talk with your mouth full.** Not one syllable, no matter how urgent.

6. **Don't chew with your mouth open.** Observe closely someone who does this and you'll understand why.

7. **Stamp out napkin abuse.** Unfold the napkin and spread it across your lap at the beginning of meal; replace it on the table at the end of the meal. In the meantime, use it to lightly dab the corners of your mouth and for no other purpose.

8. **Eliminate lipstick traces.** A woman's thing that should be eradicated from glasses and cups with tissues or cocktail napkins.

9. **Don't stow briefcases, purses, papers, etc., on table.** Anything unrelated to the dining process should be kept out of sight.

10. **Don't begin eating until everybody at the table is served.** Unless urged to by the host. Hosts should keep such urges to the minimum because people feel awkward eating when others are unserved.

11. **Don't eat too fast.** Bad for digestion, bad to watch—even at Wendy's.

12. **Don't eat too slowly.** Especially at lunch, your companions will wonder if they'll ever get back to work again.

Remember that business dining manners—from the protocol of extending the invitation to handling yourself properly at the table—represent a kind of universal language, membership in a fairly exclusive multi-cultural club. Master the fine art of business wining and dining and you can go anywhere in the world and enjoy business meals with anyone in the world. Neglect them and your dining companions may make you feel like you just got off the boat.

CONDUCT UNBECOMING AN OFFICE

How Company Manners Create
Sexual-Harassment-Free Zones

Sex is one thing that has no place in business.
                                    —EMILY POST, *ETIQUETTE* (1934)

In some situations, the line between familiarity and sexual harass-
ment is a thin one. To some, being called "honey" is business as
usual; to others it is grounds for a lawsuit.
    —MICHAEL C. THOMSETT, *THE LITTLE BLACK BOOK OF BUSINESS ETIQUETTE* (1991)

exual harassment has become a big problem for business. As we shall see, it costs business a vast amount of time and money in direct expenses and reduces the productivity of not only the harasser and the harassed, but of everyone who works with them.

The '90s workplace environment described in previous chapters—with more women and more women mangers, trilateral generational conflicts, dysfunctional office family dynamics, compromising travel circumstances—have become rich breeding grounds for harassment charges. Even state-of-the-art office equipment—risque cartoons via fax, obscene E-mail—contributes to the situation.

The second-biggest problem with sexual harassment is finding ways to keep it out or eliminate it from your office environment. The *biggest* problem is determining exactly what sexual harassment is.

I'll begin defining sexual harassment by telling you what it is not. Sexual harassment is not an occasional dirty joke or naughty word or flattering comment about a woman's appearance. Who says so? The Supreme Court in 1993. "Everyone's been walking on eggshells the last few years," said Barbara Kate Repa, author of *Sexual Harassment on the Job.* "Men wonder if they can make a joke or tell a woman she looks nice. The court is saying a little joke is okay."

It's about time. Long gone are the days when ladies could profess credible shock at profanity and men could play overgrown Boy Scouts, like John Wayne in *Stage Coach* ("Aww, gee, Miz Lil . . . Well pardon me, Ma'am.") Disingenuousness dies hard. Today's men curse like troopers then insult women with "Pardon my French" obeisances. Their counterparts are foul-mouthed harpies who cut loose and then feign genteel embarrassment.

Today, most of us swear sometimes, a lot of us even enjoy dirty jokes, and we all (no doubt) enjoy flourishing sexual lives. However jokes mean different things in different contexts. A naughty joke between "us girls" or "us guys" takes on wildly different ramifications between a man and woman. Is it merely a joke? Or is it a come-on designed to test, threaten, or thrill? The Supreme Court and I agree that whatever it may be, it is not sexual harassment, although it is also not appropriate in an office setting.

Something else sexual harassment is not is what Dr. Adele Scheele, a career strategist and *Working Woman* columnist, labels "subtle sexism." Subtle sexism includes man-made indignities that range from talking endlessly about sports, neglecting to introduce women to important clients, and accidentally on-purpose forgetting to invite women to important lunches or meetings, to claiming credit for women's ideas.

But Dr. Scheele notes, "None of these acts are illegal. No EEOC regulations have been broken, and there are no grounds for a civil suit." Subtle sexism may be dirty pool but it is not sexual harassment.

Moreover, according to the law of the land and tenets of decency, sexual harassment has nothing to do with the normal, friendly, pleasant, even mildly flirtatious banter that make workplaces worldwide a bit easier to bear. In *Sexual Harassment in the Workplace*, Ellen J. Wagner concludes, "Common courtesy, common sense, and a habit of close observation of others' reaction to what is said and done go a long way in achieving a friendly work environment where both sexes can enjoy each other's company in an atmosphere free of sexual harassment."

What *is* sexual harassment? Equal Employment Opportunity Commission Guidelines issued in 1980, affirmed by the Supreme Court in 1986, and amended by the Civil Rights Act of 1991, define sexual harassment as unwelcome sexual advances and other verbal or physical conduct of a sexual nature in which any of these three conditions apply:

- ❖ Submission to the advances or conduct are explicitly or implicitly a condition of continued employment;
- ❖ Submission to or rejection of this conduct is used as a basis for employment decisions affecting that individual; or

❖ This conduct has the purpose or intent of unreasonably interfering with an individual's work performance or creating an intimidating, hostile, or offensive working environment.

In *Step Forward, Sexual Harassment in the Workplace: What You Need to Know*, Susan L. Webb posits more concise definitions of sexual harassment, a common-sense definition, and a legal one. The common-sense or behavioral definition is "deliberate and/or repeated sexual or sex-based behavior that is not welcome, not asked for, or returned."

To qualify as illegal sexual harassment, Webb contends that the behavior must occur because of the person's sex—be related to or about sex; be unwelcome, not returned, not mutual; and affect the terms or conditions of employment, including the work environment itself.

In any event, Webb maintains that the whole issue has less to do with sex than with power. Harassers must think—consciously or otherwise—that they have the power to get away with what they're doing. Otherwise, the victim could order them to stop and it would be all over.

Whatever sexual harassment is, it has been around—in one form or another—for centuries. For instance, in the 16th century, Ivan the Terrible did it to his seven wives. In the harems of the Orient and slave plantations of the South, it was practically an automatic reflex. In the 19th-century New England mills, it was an accepted practice.

The deed may have a lengthy pedigree but the term is relatively recent. "Sexual harassment" was coined in 1975 by Cornell University instructor Lin Farley for a course entitled "Women and Work" and later used by Farley in testimony before the New York City Human Rights Commission.

In 1986 the U.S. Supreme Court ruled sexual harassment illegal. Overturning a district court decision, the Court ordered a settlement for former Meritor Savings Bank of Washington, D.C., Assistant Manager Mechelle Vinson who had been pressured into having sex by her supervisor.

In 1991 a federal court in Florida expanded the definition in its decision on the Robinson vs. Jacksonville Shipyards case. The court found that displaying nude pinups in the workplace constituted sexual harassment because it created a "hostile environment." Rejecting the company's "ostrich defense" that it was unaware of the worker's complaints, the court ordered the company to pay damages.

And 1991 was the year of the Hill/Thomas episode and the beginning of boom times for sexual harassment suits.

How much did Hill/Thomas transform the climate for sexual harassment complaints? The EEOC received between 5,603 and 6,892 complaints a year by employees in the three years before Hill/Thomas. In 1992, the year after the hearings, it received 10,578 complaints, and in the first 10 months of 1993 it received over 12,500 complaints. Also in the first 10 months of 1993, 11,000 sexual harassment cases wound up in the courts, twice as many as for all of 1990.

How pervasive is sexual harassment? A 1992 *Working Woman* survey found that 60% of its readers had personally experienced harassment, although only one quarter of them had reported it to the company. Three-quarters of the 9,000 readers who participated in the survey felt the issue of sexual harassment was as important as salary inequities, child care, and prejudice against promoting women.

The *Working Woman* survey also provides data on who's harassing and who's getting harassed. The most common scenario: a male supervisor over 35 harasses a female subordinate under 34. But nearly 30% of incidents involve women between 18 and 24, a large percentage for a small portion of the work force. *WW* also found that 83% of the time the harasser has a more powerful position in the company.

Other studies profile the typical sexual harassment victim as a woman usually between 25 and 35, and seldom over 45. Two-thirds of complainants are single, divorced, separated, or widowed; one-third are married. Over 40% are high school graduates, 12% have had some college, and 38% were college grads. Unskilled workers and those in secretarial or clerical jobs generate 51% of the complaints.

But harassment hardly vanishes when women ascend to the professions or positions of authority. "Women in managerial positions and earning over $50,000, as well as those working in male-dominated companies, are more likely to experience harassment," states *Working Woman*.

A survey by the National Association for Female Executives found that 53% of its members had been sexually harassed by men who had power over them. Nearly two-thirds of them didn't report it, and half of those who did were not satisfied with the resolution. A study of 200 female doctors in Massachusetts determined that half the general surgeons and 37% of internists had been victimized. A *National Law Journal* study found that 60% of women attorneys regarded sexual harassment at work as a "major problem."

Does sexual harassment *always* involve men harassing women? Undoubtedly not, but almost all of it does. In the summer of 1992, TV actor Gregory Harrison told a Screen Actors Guild symposium what happened when a powerful female director asked him to stop by her house to pick up a script. When Harrison declined an invitation to join her in the hot tub, she allegedly blacklisted him from seven TV series at her network.

The casting-couch role-reversal story happened in Hollywood. On Main Street men still suffer in silence: nationwide fewer than 5% of sexual harassment cases involve male victims and female harassers. Indeed, five times as many men file harassment complaints against other men.

A discriminatorily abusive work environment, even one that does not seriously affect employees' psychological well-being, can and often will detract from employees' job performance.

—SUPREME COURT JUSTICE SANDRA DAY O'CONNOR

The last word (so far) on the legal end of sexual harassment was the Supreme Court decision on November 9, 1993, in the case of Harris vs. Forklift Systems. This ruling established that men and women can tell off-color jokes in the workplace (within reason), and that men may compliment a woman's appearance (within reason). But the court also ruled *unanimously* that it was not within reason to expect a women to suffer a nervous breakdown in order to sue an employer for sexual harassment.

In his decision on the case, Supreme Court Justice Antonin Scalia wrote, "Sexual harassment is actionable if it is sufficiently severe or pervasive to alter the condition of (the victim's) employment and create an abusive work environment."

Teresa Harris, a Forklift Systems truck rental manager, didn't go crazy because her boss told her that as a woman she was too stupid to do her job, or invite her to discuss her salary at a local motel, or suggest that she slept with customers to get their business. Instead, she got mad and she sued, losing in lower courts but triumphing in the Supreme Court. The *New York Times* editorialized, "A worker has suffered enough, the Supreme Court asserts, if the employer has so polluted the workplace with sexual improprieties that a reasonable person would find it hostile and abusive, a disagreeable, unpromising place to work."

How will business respond to the challenge of maintaining what, in essence, a reasonable person would consider a civil work environment? It's too soon to tell, but many expect this latest ruling will clear up a situation long muddied by confusion and alarmism. What the decision does is make both sides less hysterical over the issue. The Court has endorsed a middle-of-the-road course. It says that sexual harassment doesn't have to drive you insane, but one dirty joke does not a lawsuit make.

The ruling should also elevate the issue out of the realm of legal gimmickry. "The Court is saying this is a serious issue," said Steven Paskoff, a former EEOC lawyer and consultant on workplace law. "They are saying, 'You better take this seriously and we aren't listening to every novel legal defense you raise.' "

In another sense it can help companies by making it easier for them to enforce their own policies against sexual harassment. Previously, a company that punished a supervisor risked a countersuit for wrongful punishment if the victim lost her case. Making it easier for victims to make their case should reduce the incidence of countersuits.

As an insurance executive, I naturally wonder how many companies are covered for sexual harassment suits. Most business liability policies don't cover it, but then it never used to be that big a problem. Up through the 1970s, awards for damages seldom exceeded a few thousand dollars.

Title VII of the Civil Rights Act of 1964 restricted awards for sexual harassment to reinstatement or front pay, up to two years of back pay, legal fees, and possible injunctive relief. Although other damages may have been available under state law, it was the Civil Rights Act of 1991 that extended the claims of victims nationwide to both compensatory and punitive damages. Punitive damages, however, are limited to a maximum amount determined not by the seriousness of the harassment but by the size of the company.

As a result of increased awareness and liberalized legislation, sexual harassment suits are proliferating. *Working Woman* found that 90% of the *Fortune* 500 companies have received sexual harassment complaints, over a third have been sued once, and a quarter have been sued repeatedly. The amounts of the awards are also headed toward the stratosphere.

- ❖ **1988.** An Oregon jury awards an executive of a moving company nearly $1.5 million for emotional distress and lost wages due to sexual advances by managers.
- ❖ **1988.** Five women in North Carolina receive a total of $3.85 million in damages resulting from sexual harassment.
- ❖ **1988.** K-Mart settles a sexual harassment charge for $3.2 million.
- ❖ **1990.** AT&T Information Systems pays a female personnel manager $2 million for sexual harassment by her supervisors.
- ❖ **1991.** A Richland, Ohio, woman receives $3.1 million because her boss made her perform oral sex to keep her job.

The insurance industry has rushed into the breach with a new type of policy. Employment-Practices Liability Insurance covers companies sued for sexual harassment for reasons of job discrimination or wrongful termination. These policies cover not only directors and officers but managers and supervisors too. Premiums vary according to the size of the company, location, and other factors. Chubb & Son sells $1 million of worth coverage for a minimum of $10,000; American International, which specializes in small companies, charges as little as $3,000 for $1 million worth of coverage for 25 employees.

But no insurance policy does or can cover the non-legal costs of harassment. *Working Woman* estimates that lower productivity, absenteeism, and higher turnover cost the average *Fortune* 500 company $6.7 million a year.

And no dollar figure can account for the lower morale and loss of pride that afflict companies which allow an atmosphere of harassment to flourish. Word gets around. Good people drift away. The best and the brightest potential personnel—those who can pick and choose where they'll work— wind up with the competition. It may not be immediately visible on the bottom line, but sexual harassment ultimately costs you plenty.

DIRTY JOKES, NUDE PICTURES, LEWD COMMENTS, PET NAMES, ADMIRING COMMENTS, REQUESTS FOR DATES: COMPANY POLICY SHOULD MAKE THEM TABOO.

Prevention is the best technique for the elimination of sexual harassment. An employer should take all steps necessary to prevent sexual harassment from occurring, such as affirmatively raising the subject, expressing strong disapproval, developing appropriate sanctions, informing employees of their right to raise the issue of harassment under Title VII, and developing methods to sensitize all concerned.

—EEOC GUIDELINES

In a perfect world you would be working for a company where everyone is treated with dignity and civility; where the golden rule governs employee interaction; where workers can cooperate, compete, disagree, even dislike one another without trying to hit each other—almost literally—below the belt. If that were the case, this chapter on sexual harassment would be a lot of white pages.

In reality, we spend a great part of our lives among flawed individuals who bring their character deficiencies to work with them. Men have sexually harassed women over the years to obtain sexual favors, exclude women from the workplace, and, failing that, obstruct their advancement. And it's worked: that's why there's been so much of it. But now, for all the legal, financial, and personnel reasons previously stated, companies must make it their business to stop sexual harassment from continuing to work.

TREAT SEXUAL HARASSMENT AS A BUSINESS ISSUE

Harassment is a business issue first, and only secondarily a woman's issue or social problem. Don't view the harassment issue as yet another hassle, imposed on you by the blankety-blank government or the blankety-blank courts. Instead, consider it a revenue-increasing/cost-cutting issue right up there with productivity, competitiveness, and benchmarking.

How do companies accomplish this? *Megatrends for Women*, which suggests that "sexual-harassment counselor" could become a hot career area for women in the '90s and beyond, says, "One way is through a lot of training, corporate 'consciousness raising' that empowers victims and potential victims, distinguishes real harassment from harmless banter, clears the air—and eventually saves the company a bundle."

Along with consultant firms in every major city, the American Management Association runs sexual harassment seminars, and most DuPont employees have been through its four-hour workshop, "A Matter of Respect." The workshop has been so well-received that a DuPont spin-off, Respect, Inc., will present the seminar to other companies.

WRITE A SEXUAL HARASSMENT POLICY

Companies that are serious formulate reasonable, thoughtful, fair-minded, very specific policies on sexual harassment. And they put it in writing. Paraphrasing Sam Goldwyn, an oral sexual harassment policy isn't worth the paper it's written on.

And it's not worth much more than the paper it's written on unless your people know what it says. The most popular ways of getting the word out include printing it in the employee handbook, posting it on bulletin boards, distributing it during workshops on the subject, and including it in the orientation package for new employees.

There are at least three good business reasons for creating a sexual harassment policy:

❖ It demonstrates management understanding and concern.

❖ It educates employees about the problem.

❖ It minimizes legal liability in the event of a lawsuit.

Policies must be tailored to the individual company and they can vary immensely, as one company might have a different set of standards than another. However, all policies should contain the following elements.

❖ **Definition.** Along with the general outline provided by the EEOC and the courts, the policy could include specific types of behavior that are considered harassment. You may include undesirable behavior that might fall short of the legal definition. Dirty jokes, nude pictures, lewd comments, pet names, admiring comments, requests for dates: company policy should make them taboo.

❖ **Resolution procedure.** Where do employees go with complaints? Not to their immediate supervisor, I hope! More often than not, the supervisor is the perpetrator of or has countenanced the harassment. Policies that send complaints to supervisors are viewed unfavorably by the EEOC and courts. According to *Sexual Harassment in the Workplace*, "Policy statements should direct inquiries and complaints on sexual harassment or other sensitive workplace

issues to a designated management ombudsman or human resources professional trained to deal with these issues and with orga-
nizational clout to resolve them."

❖ **Disciplinary action.** Statements should specify exactly what will
happen to employees who violate policy. Consequences can begin
with warnings for first offenses and stipulate an escalator of written
reprimands, letters for the employee's file, transfer, suspension, and
ultimately termination for continued infractions. Obviously, punishment must be administered fairly and even-handedly.

❖ **Good manners.** It may sound quaint compared to intricate sexual
harassment policies and prodigious forms of legal retribution. But
sexual harassment is a risk and in my mind *nothing* replaces good
manners as the most effective form of risk management. "Mind
your manners," I keep telling people, and I'm convinced that if they
did more MYM they'd need to do a lot less CYA.

In a changing and very volatile workplace, good manners are still the
best safety valve. Impeccable manners—which encompass routine daily
interaction with co-workers, style of dress, style of speech, behavior at office parties, and many other areas covered in previous chapters—can create
an aura that can render individuals virtually harassment-proof. Abuse by a
supervisor or co-worker would cause the abuser's intra-office credibility
rating to plummet the first time the abuser opened his or her mouth.

Now, I don't want anybody to think that I'm blaming the victim;
rather, I am acclaiming the non-victim.

Good manners, of course, won't stop sexual harassment any more
than burglar alarms stop burglaries. Good manners and burglar alarms only
protect those who use them and leave everyone else vulnerable.

I think sexual harassers *can* be stopped in their tracks—but only if you
change the terms of the argument. I've known plenty of men who don't
mind at all if you call them "sexists" or "male chauvinist pigs" or even
"sexual harassers." A lot them would be downright proud. However, these
same men would take deep offense if you made it a class thing and assailed
their manners.

Calling someone rude, crude, vulgar, or low-class gets them where
they live, an immeasurably more vulnerable area than the gender-sensitive
place they work. Try it some time. A well-timed "Trash!" might earn you
more workplace peace of mind than a bulletin-board-full of sexual harassment policies and a Mercedes-full of lawyers.

CIVIL WRITING
Previewing the Etiquette Book of Tomorrow

*We know only two things about the future: It cannot be known,
and it will be different from what exists now and from what
we now expect.*

—PETER DRUCKER, *MANAGING FOR RESULTS* (1990)

The future ain't what it used to be.

—YOGI BERRA (1975)

anners, like the rest of life, are in state of constant flux. Social manners change. Business manners change. Manners are living, breathing things that reflect new aspects of the behavior manners aspire to regulate.

Don't believe me? Here are two events involving real-world etiquette that recently caught my eye.

In an article on "the new street etiquette," *New York Times Magazine* reporter Molly O'Neill describes seeing a well-dressed 20-something businesswoman sit down on a curb in midtown Manhattan. She proceeds to take off the jacket of her business suit, pull on a pair of shiny lycra tights under her Liz Claiborne skirt, don kneepads, thick socks, and Rollerblades, and then skates into the rush-hour traffic.

The point of etiquette, however, wasn't that the absence of phone booths and public restrooms make it acceptable now for people to change clothes in the street. It was about the reaction of passersby. "The sidewalk is crowded, but no one seems to notice. People have learned not to look. Oddly, in an age that shuns decorum, *common courtesy* [italics mine] has replaced structural walls."

The reporter notes that the etiquette of the averted glance also applies to people at ATM machines and nursing mothers. "In each case the ob-server, not the performer, is in bad taste. This nuance of etiquette used to be reserved for the less fortunate . . . But the disappearance of time and space is changing that. Looking the other way has become a middle-class way of life."

The other case of mutating manners is an etiquette guide for beggars prepared by a homeless advocacy group in Baltimore. Entitled "A Guide for the Polite Panhandler," the brochure tenders the following tips:

- ❖ Try to make eye contact, recognizing the humanity of the panhandled.
- ❖ Always say "Please" and "Thank you."
- ❖ Never follow or yell at people; harassment is illegal.
- ❖ Do not block the sidewalk or interfere with commercial businesses.
- ❖ Offering to work for food is frequently effective.
- ❖ Smile—you can catch more flies with honey than with vinegar.
- ❖ Never use profane language.
- ❖ Remember, everyone has the right to say no.

Actually, except for the stuff about blocking sidewalks and working for food, this would be pretty good business etiquette for people in any line of work.

❧❧❧

The business manners of tomorrow can be divided into two categories. One category deals with manners involving *technology*—new machines, office equipment, computers, procedures, and processes that are already infiltrating our work lives. The other category involves *workstyles* and include telecommuting, job sharing, parental leave, working fathers, and other developments in personnel management.

What new technology and new workstyles have in common are that they are all introduced to improve efficiency, productivity, and morale. What they also have in common are that they perplex the people who have to learn to deal with them. Hence the need for a new set of rules. Let's begin with the easy part, new technology.

Picturephones

Does anyone really want a telephone that lets you look at, in Lily Tomlin's phrase, the party to whom you are speaking? Maybe, but does anybody want *them* to see *you*. Well, Ma Bell and her extended family are committed to the concept and what Ma Bell wants, Ma Bell ultimately gets.

How will it work? Presumably, the phone rings and the person who answers immediately goes on camera. If someone answers the phone for you, you are blessed with a buffer zone. Men can leave the caller on hold while they comb their hair, adjust their ties, slip on a suit jacket. Women can check their clothes, hair, and make-up. How long is too long to keep the caller on hold? I say that 15–30 seconds is reasonable and decent. That may not sound like enough now, but once you get the hang of it—and get the hang of it you will when you do it 50 times a day—it'll go much faster.

Once on camera, make like Dan Rather or Connie Chung. Look into the camera—don't let your gaze wander or stare blankly into space. Facial expressions must respond to the conversation. Laugh if your caller says something funny; nod gravely to communicate deep concern. It's fine if they see you taking notes, not so good if you're spotted glancing at a magazine or playing a Gameboy. Most vital to remember when using a picturephone: keep fingers far away from mouth and nose.

E-Mail

Electronic mail will become an increasingly important element in the business of tomorrow. Most major corporations are already equipped to send and receive mail via computer and modem. Even the White House, never before glimpsed on the cutting edge of new technology, is set up to receive E-Mail from the public.

But E-Mail can also program a lot of inter-office grief. An E-Mail contretemps arose at the headquarters of the National Science Foundation in Washington when one male official bleeped a three-page story entitled "Impure Mathematix" that inscrtcd abstruse mathematical terms in place of pornographic ones. A typical phrase: "Quite suddenly two branches of hyperbola touched her at a single point. She oscillated violently . . ."

Female scientists who got the message were not amused. The naughty nerd who sent it claimed the story just materialized in his E-Mailbox one morning (as E-Mail will do). When he tried to delete it, he accidentally mailed it to the entire staff. The women didn't buy it. They instead assumed he was trying to send it to his buddies, but that it somehow wound up in everybody's mailbox (as E-Mail will do). Bad feelings still reign at NSF.

E-Mail is actually one of the most inherently polite forms of communication ever invented. Computers automatically and instantly acknowledge receipt of your message. How many of your friends and business associates are so thoughtful?

But don't let your E-Mail zap you in the back. E-Mail is not personal mail and it's not Dear Diary: it's an open book to anyone who cracks the code. It's no place for pornography, sexist slights, ethnic slurs, expressions of fanatical political partisanship. It's the wrong context for hatching plots against management, discussing job offers from competitors, or disclosing anything else you don't want the whole world to know.

Don't try sending anonymous missives either: E-Mail always leaves electronic fingerprints. Keep messages brief and to the point. And if you absolutely cannot resist transmitting the latest topical joke, make sure the joke you E-Mail is a clean one.

Future Fashions

Futurists are convinced that many of us will *wear* the office of tomorrow. One form of body office now under development by the NEC Corporation in Tokyo is a soft plastic "lap body computer" worn like a shield over the chest. Unfolded for use it resembles an airplane snack tray attached to you, rather than to seat in front of you. Weighing only 2.2 pounds and held to the body by velcro straps, the lap body computer recognizes voice and handwriting and incorporates keyboards, telephones, display screens, faxes, CD memories. It will do everything an office full of equipment will do anywhere you want to do it.

Obviously, new rules are needed to govern this radical development of apparel/equipment. Color, for example. I recommend subdued conservative tones, about the same shades recommended for job interview suits. Is it proper to post messages on the front of the lap body computer? Perhaps, but nothing tacky like your home phone number or an ad for a pizza parlor. A company logo may be acceptable. Lap body computers, even black ones, are *never* proper dress for evening affairs. Don't open them in elevators, crowded commuter trains, or in any setting where small children are running around underfoot.

Further along, all the capabilities of the lap body computer will be condensed into a wrist-band unit Dick Tracy would die for. Computer screen and telephone will be built into a pair of wraparound sunglasses. The small size and relative inconspicuousness of these units eliminates most problems of decorum. However, it will always be rude to wear your wristband and shades during business meetings, at the theater, or at formal dinner parties.

⚜

The rest of *Etiquette 2000* would address the changing human dynamics of the workplace—the workstyles. As noted in previous chapters, the rising number of working women will force even more companies to deal with issues like childcare, flextime, and job sharing. Now, men are getting into the parental leave and childcare act. And of course accommodation must be made for the young Generation Three types whose work habits are less motivated by ambition than by desire to balance worklife and homelife.

Most of the workstyles of the future already exist in experimental or pilot programs. The smart money says they're bound to spread.

Telecommuting

Today's technology of computers, modems, faxes, and versatile phone systems make it quite feasible for employees to go to work and at the same time stay at home. Employees like to telecommute because they don't have to spend time and money on real commuting; they don't get bogged down in office socializing, politicking, and other distractions; and they actually get more work done. If they're parents, they get to spend more time with their kids.

Employers like telecommuting because it saves the cost of office space and related costs of having employees on hand, it often raises productivity, and it boosts the morale and loyalty of employees who choose to work this way. Everybody likes it, but a code of etiquette is necessary to make sure everybody gets what they want.

TELECOMMUTER DRESS CODE

I don't expect men to put on a suit and tie, but you should shave and wear something a bit more decorous than a sweat suit or shorts and T-shirt. And you should wear shoes—not slippers, real shoes. Telecommuting women can eschew stockings and heels, but light make-up and a reasonably attractive outfit—perhaps something you would wear to go out shopping—are suitable. Believe it or not, people who work at home report that the better they're dressed, the more efficiently they function. So don't wear rags, but save your best outfits for periodic forays into the office.

TELECOMMUTER TECHNOLOGY

Most telecommuters install separate phone lines for business. Calls on this line are answered in a businesslike way they've worked out with their boss: "Ace Enterprises, Tony Telecommuter speaking." You don't have to answer the business phone outside of business hours—and you *shouldn't* answer your private line during business hours. Get answering machines to do all that. You'll also need a fax, a computer and printer, modem, possibly a photocopying machine—and phone numbers of people who can come out to repair it all at a moment's notice.

WORKDAY

Telecommuters observe the same business hours as the gang at the office. If that means nine-to-five, you are on-duty during that entire period. Time off for breaks and lunch are included in the telecommuter bill of rights. Shopping, dental appointments, and naps take unfair advantage of the situation. If you leave your post to take care of personal matters, inform the office and arrange to make up the time after-hours or over the weekend.

TELECOMMUTER KIDS

Children should not be seen, nor should they be heard. During the workday you are theoretically in the office (albeit one where the boss won't surprise you and co-workers don't stop by to chat). Children don't belong in offices, and telecommuting is not company-supported childcare. No one does serious work in a house where children are present but unaccounted for. Bring in someone to watch your kids or take them to childcare. The advantage of telecommuting for parents is not that you can spend all day with your children, but that you get more time with them at the beginning, middle, and at the end of the day.

DURING THE WORKDAY, YOU ARE THEORETICALLY IN THE OFFICE. CHILDREN DON'T BELONG IN OFFICES AND TELECOMMUTNG IS NOT COMPANY-SUPPORTED CHILDCARE.

Job Sharing

Job sharing is another idea whose star is rising. In fact, 16% of U.S. companies already use job sharing as a way to increase flexibility.

Companies like job sharing for the same reason people like Doublemint gum: twice the experience, energy, and creative input for a single salary. The appeal for job sharers is that they can get a job with full-time stature and per hour/diem pay, and work only a part-time schedule.

Job shares are often compared to marriages: they succeed by blending people who have much in common but aren't *exactly* alike. Job shares, like marriages, work when the pair has similar attitudes toward the job and about work itself. Job partners should have similar expectations, they should not excessively compete with one another, and they should be thoroughly honest with each other. Like successful marriages, they need to communicate clearly and bring complementary and supplementary skills into the relationship. And just like a marriage, job shares present a lot of tricky issues work out.

WHO DOES WHAT? Usually the pay and work are divided 50-50. But is it 50-50 in terms of time in the office, number of clients, or according to some other criteria? How will you be compensated if you collectively exceed the requirements of a single job?

WHO GOES WHERE? If both of you show up at meetings, how do you compensate the one who's off-duty when the meeting takes place? What kind of attention do you give clients and other outside contacts? Separate-but-equal or buy-one-get-one-free? Job sharers don't have to answer to each other's names, but they do have to take calls and otherwise respond to situations that their partners routinely handle.

WHAT HAPPENS WHEN A PARTNER LEAVES? Is the job share automatically terminated, or can the surviving partner get an opportunity to find a replacement? In most cases, the company re-evaluates the job share program to determine whether it will continue.

New daddies need paternity leave like they need a hole in the head.

—MALCOLM FORBES (1986)

Working Fathers

Remember the "Mommy Track"? It became a big buzzword in the 1980s when it was disclosed that certain companies divided female workers into "career-primary women" headed straight up the corporate ladder and "family-oriented women" condemned to second-rate jobs and pay. Family-oriented women were said to be on the Mommy Track, a slow track headed practically nowhere.

What's new in the '90s and surely decades to come is the advent of the Daddy Track, so-called "working fathers" who eschew the fast track in favor of flexible, lower-paying jobs that give them more time for families and outside pursuits. You haven't heard *too* much about them yet because very few of them exist—or are willing to admit it.

There are several reasons why that's bound to change. One is lowered career expectations. According to the *New York Times*, "Men who are now 30 to 60 years old are the first U.S. generation to be less successful than their fathers at the same age . . . This economic decline has caused men to reevaluate work in a harsh new light."

Part of the harsh light is reflected off the women who are grabbing the kind of upper-level jobs men traditionally deemed their birthright. Unreasonably but somewhat understandably, men get resentful and discouraged when jobs they covet go to more qualified females.

And then there are the Generation Three guys who are happy to swap the gray flannel suit and briefcase for a sweat suit and gym bag—or even a diaper bag. Such men, it is rumored, even perform a considerable amount of the housework, although not even the most optimistic observers believe their contributions in this realm will ever approach parity.

How should management and co-workers treat working dads? With consideration, respect, courtesy, and decency—exactly the same way they treat everybody else. If Daddy Trackers are not accorded the deference and attentiveness granted go-getters of either sex destined for positions of authority, it is an understandable consequence of the choice they have made. They've made their beds, now they have to . . . do laundry, shop for groceries, pick up the kids at school, etc.

Daddy Trackers must behave with comparable consideration towards employers and co-workers—and they should start during the job interview. Yes, you want the job and don't want to reveal anything that might lose it for you. But it's only fair play to lay your Daddy-Track cards on the table. Tell the interviewer you're qualified for the job, will work your head off at it, but that family comes first. You want your nights and weekends to yourself. And during the work week, on very rare occasions, emergencies may come up that you will have to leave work to handle. Yes, truth-in-advertising may cost you the job. But the job you get will be a job you can keep.

On-the-job decency starts with the event that makes men working dads—the birth of a child. More and more fathers are taking paternity leave. Entire books have been written to shepherd women through the process, but there is little guidance for fathers. For men, fortunately, the situation is considerably less complicated.

In the first place, while women often begin their leave a week or two before the due date, there's no good reason for men to leave until just prior to birth. How much time should he take off? The Family Leave Act mandates up to 12 weeks of unpaid leave for government employees or employees in large companies. However, men who ride the Daddy Track that far may quickly reach the end of the line. Probably, three to six weeks is plenty of time, longer than a vacation but shorter than a disappearing act.

Before taking maternity/paternity leave, men and women should put all their business affairs in order. Make hard-copy or computerized summaries of everything you're working on, including phone numbers of important clients. Be sure everyone in the office knows you're just on leave, not retired or otherwise inaccessible. You are definitely available *at any time* to answer questions by phone or even come into work to deal with urgent situations.

Mommy/Daddy Trackers will undoubtedly go to the front of the line to take advantage of previously discussed flextime options like telecommuting and job sharing. In conventional work situations, balancing family and job mainly involves a lot of advance planning and crystal-clear communication. Let your boss and co-workers know well in advance when you need a long lunch to take Billy to the dentist or must leave on the dot of five for Cindy's soccer match. And make sure they know when and how you'll make up the lost time.

Times change. Manners change. However, the need to have manners never changes. No, manners can't work miracles, and they may always be destined to be a bit out of date. Still, our manners are among the best things we have until our minds truly change and our morals catch up.

The poet John Keats wrote, "Beauty is truth, truth beauty,—that is all ye know on earth, and all ye need to know." Er, not quite, John. At bottom, manners are as basic and as moral as the Golden Rule. Still, it would be poetic injustice to pretend that was simply the end of the matter.

Let's face a hard but undeniable fact: Even the best workplaces are necessarily tense places. In a supposedly classless society, they're one of the only places where we are overtly judged and ranked and where we voluntarily defer to power.

To be decent in such trying circumstances, let alone gracious, requires considerable tact and grace. But grace never goes unnoticed. For that matter, those who build up a reserve of good will don't get blasted for social mistakes—especially if it's obvious that he or she is trying.

The reason for this in universal. Just as people hate phoniness, arrogance, and selfishness, they prize decency, the purest of human gold. That much will never change. Decency is irresistible: *that's* all you need to know.

How To Weave Your Way Through The Social Fabric
Of Today's Swiftly Changing Workplace

UNCIVIL WARS:

A Survival Guide For Men and Women in the Office of the 90s

❖ How are we supposed to behave at work when the rules for men and women seem to be changing all the time?

❖ If it's okay at a party, why not at the office?

❖ Should I let him kiss me or insist on a handshake?

BEVERLY H. PATRICK says the answer to such social-business problems is as old as culture and as new as today's styles:

— IT'S MANNERS —

An acknowledged leader in corporate America, Beverly as a public speaker combines insight with wisdom, hilarious examples with painful memories. She serves audiences a rich stew of manners as the saving grace in today's workplace—for men and women, young and old, employers and employees.

Her entertaining presentations, whether as main event keynotes, luncheon speeches, brief after-dinner talks or seminars followed by spirited colloquy with audiences, never fail to amuse, inform, and excite her listeners.

Beverly personally inspires younger professionals with her career example. As president and chief executive officer of a national insurance services firm, she has arrived at the pinnacle of what is traditionally a man's preserve.

While working with professional liability insurance issues, especially medical malpractice, Beverly became an authority on manners in business while rising to the top. Today she enjoys sharing her keen perspective with a variety of business and professional audiences. Speaking to audiences nationwide on the subject of manners in the workplace is easy for Beverly. She calls manners "the oldest form of risk management."

Beverly has more than two decades of experience working with clients on national and international levels. She regularly speaks at meetings across the U.S. and Canada and is the author of numerous articles in national business magazines and trade publications.

To contact Beverly for a presentation to your group or for more information:

Beverly H. Patrick
108-74th Street
Virginia Beach, VA 23451
Telephone/Fax (804) 422-3764

SELECTED BIBLIOGRAPHY

Aburdene, Patricia & Naisbitt, John. *Megatrends for Women*. New York: Villard Books, 1992.

Adams, Michael. "Tea Formation." *Successful Meetings*, October, 1993.

Baldridge, Letitia. *Letitia Baldridge's New Corporate Guide to Executive Manners*. New York: Rawson Associates, 1993.

Barbieri, Susan M. "How to Win Allies and Influence Snakes." *Working Woman*, August, 1993.

Crichton, Sarah. "Sexual Correctness: Has it gone too far?" *Newsweek*, October 25, 1993.

DeVries, Mary A. *The Complete Office Handbook*. New York: Signet, 1987.

Dunckel, Jacqueline. *Business Etiquette Today: A Guide to Corporate Success*. Vancouver: Self-Counsel Press, 1987.

Edwards, Owen. *Upward Nobility*. New York: Crown, 1991.

Eichler, Lillian. *Book of Etiquette*. New York: Doubleday, 1923.

Eichler, Lillian. *The New Book of Etiquette*. Garden City, NY: Garden City Publishing Company, 1924, 1934 eds.

Ford, Charlotte. *Etiquette: Charlotte Ford's Guide to Modern Manners.* New York: Clarkson N. Potter, 1988.

Hardesty, Sarah & Jacobs, Nehama. *Success and Betrayal.* New York: Simon & Schuster, 1987.

Harvey, Gordon E. & Lee, II, Edward L. *Doing Business in the United States.* McLean, Va.: Business Travel Books, 1992.

Hill, Thos. E. *Hill's Manual of Social and Business Forms: A Guide to Correct Writing.* Chicago: Moses Warren & Co., 1878.

Holt, Emily. *Encyclopedia of Etiquette.* Garden City, NY: Doubleday, Page, 1911.

Howe, Neil, & Strauss, William. "The New Generation Gap." *The Atlantic,* December, 1992.

King, Julie Adair. *The Smart Woman's Guide to Interviewing and Salary Negotiation.* Hawthorne, N.J.: Career Press, 1993.

King, Julie Adair & Sheldon, Betsy. *The Smart Woman's Guide to Resumes and Job Hunting.* Hawthorne, N.J.: Career Press, 1991.

Lawlor, Julia. "Generation gap: Busters seek balanced work life." *USA Today,* November 14, 1993.

Lundin, William & Lundin, Kathleen. *The Healing Manager.* San Francisco: Berrett-Koehler Publishers, 1993.

Martin, Judith. *Miss Manners' Guide to the Turn-of-the-Millennium.* New York: Pharos Books, 1989.

Mauro, Tony. "Court clears air on sexual harassment." *USA Today,* November 10, 1993.

Mazzei, George. *The New Office Etiquette.* New York: Poseidon Press, 1983.

McDowell, Edwin. "Traveling More on Business, Women Seek More of Hotels." *New York Times,* June 17, 1992.

Mendelsohn, Jennifer. "Talking? About a new way of talking?" *USA Today,* November 2, 1993.

Molloy, John T. *The Woman's Dress For Success Book.* New York: Warner Books, 1977.

Monroe, Valerie. "Men and Women." *Mirabella,* December 1992.

Naisbitt, John & Aburdene, Patricia. *Megatrends 2000.* New York: William Morrow, 1990.

O'Rourke, P.J. *Modern Manners: An Etiquette Book for Rude People.* New York: Atlantic Monthly Press, 1991.

Post, Elizabeth L. *Emily Post's Etiquette.* New York: Harper & Row, 1984.

Post, Emily. *Etiquette: The Blue Book of Social Usage.* New York: Funk & Wagnalls, 1937

Rosiere, Gabrielle. *Etiquette: An Encyclopedia of Good Manners and Social Usage.* New York: Edward J. Clode, 1923.

Sandroff, Ronni. "Sexual Harassment: The Inside Story." *Working Woman,* June 1992.

Scheele, Dr. Adele. "Subtle Sexism." *Working Woman,* July 1992.

Stewart, Marjabelle Young. *The New Etiquette: Real Manners of Real People in Real Situations—An A-To-Z Guide.* New York: St. Martin's, 1987.

Thomsett, Michael C. *The Little Black Book of Business Etiquette.* New York: AMACOM, 1991.

Van Hulsteyn, Peggy. *What Every Business Woman Needs To Know To Get Ahead.* New York: Dodd, Mead, 1984.

Wagner, Ellen J. *Sexual Harassment In The Workplace.* New York: Amacom, 1992.

Women's Changing Role. Wylie, TX: Information Plus, 1990.

World Almanac 1994. New York: Pharos Books, 1993.

Worthington, E.R. & Worthington, Anita E. *People Investment.* Grant's Pass, OR: Oasis Press, 1993.

Webb, Susan L. *Step Forward: Sexual Harassment in the Workplace: What You Need To Know!* New York: MasterMedia, 1991.

Wyden, Peter. "Sexual Harassment." *Good Housekeeping,* July 1993.

Wyse, Lois. *Company Manners.* New York: Crown, 1992.

Yager, Jan. *Business Protocol.* New York: John Wiley & Sons, 1991.